THE
SUPREME COURT
IN
AMERICAN HISTORY
Ten Great Decisions

THE
SUPREME COURT
IN
AMERICAN
HISTORY

TEN GREAT DECISIONS
*The People, The Times and
The Issues*

MARJORIE G. FRIBOURG

Macrae Smith Company : Philadelphia

ACKNOWLEDGMENTS

The author would like to express her special thanks to Mr. Mark Woolsey, Managing Editor of *United States Law Week,* for his helpful editorial suggestions and for the time and interest he devoted to the manuscript.

She remembers, too, with sincere appreciation the many helpful librarians, lawyers and litigants interviewed in the course of writing this book.

FOREWORD

The Supreme Court is the conscience of the Constitution. No more powerful voices in its defense can be raised in the land than those of the nine black-robed justices whose decisions affect the lives of everyday Americans in ways that the Founding Fathers never envisioned. The ten great cases examined in this book disclose the Constitution of the United States to be a living fabric, not a frozen parchment. With some notable exceptions, the occupants of the highest bench, from Chief Justice Marshall down to Chief Justice Warren, have sought to carry out the spirit of the Constitution and to make that charter respond to the changing needs of American society.

John Marshall saw to it that the national power was exercised in the national interest as the Constitution intended. The present Court under Chief Justice Warren is providing continued assurance that the rights of all Americans, regardless of race or creed, are protected; that the accused shall be given a fair trial; and that our society shall be truly democratic, one in which each man's vote shall count as much as another's.

Each of the ten great decisions freshly considered in this book cover some different facet of the Court's function in carrying out the national will. In these pages one meets towering jurists like Marshall, Storey, Taney, Holmes, and Brandeis. One hears able lawyers like Daniel Webster, James A. Garfield, and Thurgood Marshall, and one learns how difficult and controversial issues are finally resolved by the Court.

It is the special virtue of this book that it makes technical issues relatively simple. Whether we are reading about the commerce clause, or the implied powers of the Constitution, or the vested rights of property, or the issue of monopoly, or of desegregation, or the separation of church and state, we find the exposition lucid and we reach the point of the case quickly. These cases are not theoretical. They were brought to the Court by real people with real problems. Mrs. Fribourg never forgets the human issues, while at the same time she never lets the Constitutional questions get swamped in a welter of technical details. *The Supreme Court in American History,* in its case-by-case approach, provides insights into the working of the highest Court in the land that will reward and enrich the reader and give a new dimension to his knowledge of our Constitutional system.

RICHARD B. MORRIS

Gouverneur Morris Professor of History
Columbia University

CONTENTS

CASE 9   *School District of Abington Township* v.
           Schempp

CASE 10   *Baker* v. *Carr*

APPENDIX

INTRODUCTION

In 1893 the famous English historian, statesman and jurist James Bryce wrote about the United States court system in his widely acclaimed book *The American Commonwealth,* "Few American institutions are better worth studying . . . few deserve more admiration . . . There is no part of the American system which reflects more credit on its authors."

Like most Europeans, Bryce marveled at the independence and power vested in the United States judiciary. Its judges are appointed for life, during good behavior. They cannot be removed without cause—by whim of the legislature or the executive. Even more remarkable is the fact that through their power to interpret the Constitution, the justices of the Supreme Court can void an act of the states or an act of Congress. This power to overturn a law passed by the legislature was unique on earth when the Founding Fathers gave it to the United States' highest court. Chief Justice John Marshall later explained that the Founding Fathers had given this power to the Court by making the Constitution, which the justices were to interpret, the supreme law of the land.

Besides having this tremendous power, the justices of the Supreme Court can side with an individual in his struggle for justice against a department of the executive, for the constitutional interpretations made by the justices are superior to either ordinary law or executive order.

The Court was designed by the Founding Fathers to keep the states, the Congress and the President within the bounds of their stated powers in order to preserve the Constitution. They made the Constitution difficult to amend because it was there that they stated those broad principles which they intended to protect the common citizen from tyranny by either the Government or the majority of the people. They then left it up to the Court to see that these principles of liberty and justice for all were never violated. Thus, the Supreme Court often becomes the community's conscience. As it controls neither the Government's purse nor its sword, it relies mostly on the force of its moral judgment, its legal and traditional prestige and the educational impact of its words to compel obedience to its dictates.

When the Supreme Court rules, it makes its decision on a specific lawsuit brought before it. These suits are started by men and women whose struggles often reflect the conflicts of their times. If possible, the high Court settles the controversy by stating what an ordinary law means or how it applies. Only when absolutely necessary do the justices hand down a new interpretation of the Constitution. But on those momentous occasions when the Court does add to the volume of judicial decisions on the meaning of the Constitution, it thereby alters the ways of the Government and of the people and thus alters the course of history.

The stories that follow describe ten famous cases that came before the Supreme Court. They tell the tales of the men and women who waged these legal battles, the difficulties they faced, the triumphs and despair they experienced. In each case the Court had to interpret the Constitution in order to render justice, thus shaping the ideas of government by which we live today.

THE
SUPREME COURT
IN
AMERICAN HISTORY
Ten Great Decisions

☆ CASE 1 ☆

Marbury v. Madison

A Fighting Chief Justice
Asserts the Authority of the Court

"It is emphatically the province and duty of the judicial department to say what the law is."

JOHN MARSHALL, 1803

THE TIMES
AND THE ISSUES

Today the voice of the United States Supreme Court rings with authority. This was not always so. When the nation was young the country's highest tribunal entrusted with interpreting the Constitution had to battle its way toward might and dignity.

It was in 1803, during the early precarious period of the Court's history, that it heard the strange case of William Marbury (Justice of the Peace) v. James Madison (Secretary of State). The justices had to face both the problem and the consequences of their decision. Dared they? Was this the time to establish their power to nullify an unconstitutional law passed by Congress?

Had the Court not acted, future laws might have demolished the Constitution and with it the nation's hard-won system of unity and self-government. Here is what led up to the quarrel and how it took place.

☆

". . . *The Next Will Be Drawn in Blood*"

A crowd converged in the meeting hall of Richmond's new Academy Building on Monday, June 2, 1788. Struggling through the throng to reach their seats were 168 state-elected delegates. These men were judges, lawyers, clergymen, farmers and rugged frontiersmen. They had come over dusty roads by horse and by wagon from every corner of the state, roused by the results of an earlier meeting called in Philadelphia at which a Constitution was drafted for the whole United States. Now they were assembling before the excited spectators to determine whether Virginia—the most heavily populated state in America—should approve and adopt the Constitution, sacrificing some of her own independence.

Among the delegates was an emaciated young man with dark hair and dark eyes, whose coat and breeches hung loosely over his long frame, giving him an almost disheveled appearance. He was John Marshall, an attorney and a veteran of the Revolution, who was determined that the Constitution should be adopted and that a strong court should be created to uphold it. Anxiously he watched while fiery Patrick Henry held the floor.

Henry thundered the sentiments of many. Why, he asked, let the new Constitution create a super-authority over the States? "Tyranny!" Henry called it, and held both the chambers and galleries spellbound with his oratory.

After Henry's eloquence, John Marshall and his colleagues James Madison and Edmund Pendleton argued their point for twenty-three days. They declared that separate states were helpless to promote the people's welfare, stop the commercial warring between the states, make the states keep the nation's treaties with the Indians and the British, or even provide for the country's defense.

Marshall, who had been a soldier at Valley Forge, knew that heavy losses had prolonged the Revolution because the states, being independent, contributed only what they wished for food, clothing, blankets and ammunition.

He climaxed his speech with an old battle cry. "United we are strong, divided we fall!" he said, and added, ". . . it requires a superintending power to call forth the resources of all to protect all." Since the government of that time—the Confederation—was nothing but a weak league of divided states, it lacked, he argued, the vigor for survival.

As for Henry's cry of tyranny, Marshall declared that the new Constitution secured justice in a manner that was new to the world.

Besides limiting the powers of the President and the legislature, the Constitution made the judiciary an independent branch of the Government. If Congress were to pass a tyrannical law, "They [the Supreme Court justices] would declare it void. . . . There is no other body that can afford such protection," Marshall said.

Still, the listening men were fearful and loath to cede their local powers. When the ayes and the nays were counted, the delegates passed the Constitution by the frighteningly narrow margin of ten votes. With so much opposition and so much misunderstanding, the Constitution might yet be lost—its tenets violated or ignored. General Washington had predicted that should this excellent Constitution be canceled, "the next will be drawn in blood." It would take a forceful Court to prevent that, Marshall realized. The fight was not yet finished.

But for the next decade and a half the Supreme Court was pitifully without prestige. Men refused to be appointed justices and some, after accepting appointment, soon left for other posts.

Marshall, deeply concerned, supported the Federalist party because it stood for strengthening the branches of the Federal government. As time passed, his influence increased, although at first not in connection with the Court. In 1797, he was ambassador to France; in 1799, he was Congressman Marshall; in 1800, President John Adams made him his Secretary of State.

Then, in the next November elections, Adams and the Federalists were defeated by the political group led by Thomas Jefferson.

Jefferson's followers were called Republicans, sometimes Democratic Republicans, and years later would name themselves the Democratic party. They wanted political power left in the hands of the states, with little Federal interference, and therefore, they wanted a weak Court. Since they were to take office March 4, it was obvious to Marshall that if anything was ever to be done to infuse life into the Supreme Court, it would have to be done within the next three months, or tradition and precedent would be forever against it. The Court would then remain helpless—unable, when necessary, to rescue the Constitution and the Union.

At that moment—November, 1800—the Supreme Court did not even have a place to meet. Washington, D.C., had been the country's capital for over half a year but Marshall was still writing to the District Commissioners, responsible for public buildings, asking what arrangement could be made for housing the Court.

In December a new complication arose. President Adams received a letter from Oliver Ellsworth, the Chief Justice of the Supreme Court, and announced to his intimates that "Mr. Ellsworth, afflicted with the gravel and the gout and intending to pass the winter in the South of France . . . has resigned his office."

Marshall hoped to seize this opportunity to bolster the Court. He urged President Adams to appoint a vigorous Chief Justice. Associate Justice William Paterson of New Jersey, he argued, should be promoted to fill the vacancy.

Secretary of State Marshall had good reason to hope that the President might accept his recommendations, for Adams himself, while examining the Republican position, had stated, "In the future administration of our country, the finest security we can have is a solid Judiciary." Besides, although Adams was in a foul mood and furious at over half his associates for criticizing him before and during his Presidential campaign, Marshall still enjoyed his highest esteem. Other politicians admiringly commented, "The President obeys his Secretary of State without suspecting it."

This time Adams surprised them. He did not appoint Paterson, but offered the post to John Jay of New York. Jay had been Chief Justice once before—he had been Washington's first appointment —but he had quit the job six years before.

Marshall, disappointed, must have wondered how Jay, now an old man, could endure the rigors of riding circuit that the job entailed. Each Supreme Court justice, by Act of Congress, was assigned a circuit, or area, through which he was forced to spend months each year bouncing over rough country roads in a horse-drawn carriage, because his job was to sit beside the judges of the widely scattered lower courts and hear cases with them. Most often, after an exhausting journey or a day in court, a Supreme Court justice had to put up for the night at some evil-smelling tavern.

The system riled Marshall. He had explained to Adams that the justices resented this extra duty. Besides, they occasionally had to listen to the same cases for a second time, for cases were sometimes reviewed before the high tribunal. How could an individual justice be expected to weigh the arguments impartially a second time? He had already made his decision.

At Marshall's insistence, Adams, in his last message to the dying Congress, did recommend reform. Should the debating Congressmen pass the reform bill called the Judiciary Act of 1801, sixteen new circuit judges would be appointed by the President. That would end circuit riding as an impediment to the High Court's effectiveness and prestige.

However, the fact that circuit duty had to continue in the interim was to prove a stroke of good luck for his cause. Shortly before the twentieth of January, Jay's answer to the President's offer reached Washington. According to custom, the message was sent through John Marshall because he was Secretary of State. Jay's concluding sentence complained that the state of his health "was incompetent to the fatigues incident to the office"—i.e., circuit riding.

Marshall took the letter and trudged down muddy Pennsylvania Avenue to the White House. Inside the still sparsely furnished Executive Mansion, Secretary and President respectfully, even affectionately, faced each other.

Mr. Adams, short, plump and excitable, fashionably dressed with a fluffy ruffle under his full chin, was a scholarly attorney with a Harvard degree. His admiration for his Secretary of State was an example of the attraction of opposites. Marshall, in spite of having risen to high office, was still the product of his frontier upbringing. He was careless of his dress, and often, hungering for a breath of fresh air, he tramped to his appointments on foot, arriving windblown, with shoes muddied. Lacking Adams' formal education, he nevertheless had a genius for calm, logical thinking and a firm, good-natured manner, which inspired the confidence of other men.

Marshall waited while the President read what Jay had written: "I left [the Court] perfectly convinced it . . . would not obtain the energy, weight and dignity which are essential to its affording due support to the nation's government."

When Adams looked up from the paper, he asked, "Whom shall I nominate now?"

"I cannot say," Marshall replied, "since I suppose your objection to Paterson remains."

"I shall not nominate him," Adams snapped. Then there must have been a silence before the President added, thoughtfully, "I believe I must nominate you." *

Marshall, stunned, bowed his head. His name had been mentioned for the presidency but never in connection with the Court. Yet because his greatest concern was the preservation of the Constitution, he realized that this office meant even more to him than the presidency.

The two men parted knowing that they must wait to see if the Senate would confirm Marshall's appointment. In the weeks that followed, Marshall's earlier efforts bore fruit. The District Commissioners wrote to the Congress asking if "the Supreme Court may be accommodated with a room in the Capitol to hold its sessions." Congress selected a tiny, twenty-two–foot room on the ground floor. Then, while this was being converted into a courtroom, Congress passed the Judiciary reform bill and—most important of all —the Senate confirmed Marshall as Chief Justice. The fight for a stronger Court was now Marshall's own.

He wrote to the President, "I shall enter immediately into the duties of the office, and hope never to give you occasion to regret having made the appointment." Then, clothed in a black robe, he went to the tiny courtroom and stood before the five other justices. They, together with the Chief Justice, made up the bench, or Court, in those days. And before them John Marshall took the oath of office.

After all that, President Adams' reply to Marshall's letter of acceptance must have been a shock: "The circumstances of the times . . . render it necessary that I must request and authorize you . . . to continue to discharge all the duties of Secretary of State." Adams did not want to appoint a new Secretary of State to serve for only two weeks.

Holding two offices would not have been so exasperating for Marshall if Congress had not passed an act providing the capital

---

* The foregoing dialogue was described in a letter later written by Marshall to Justice Story. The existence of this letter was for many years unknown, but today a photostat of it can be seen in the little book *An Autobiographical Sketch* by *John Marshall*, edited by J. Stokes Adams. The original letter is in the William L. Clements Library at the University of Michigan.

area with forty-two justices of the peace (minor judges) who were to serve for five years. Adams wanted to appoint all of them before he went out of office, so every day Marshall had to write out commissions for the President's signature and stamp them with the Great Seal of the United States. He was well aware that Adams distrusted the incoming Republicans, but he was also conscious that Jefferson's men were jeering at this last-minute method of putting defeated Federalists on the public pay roll. "Midnight Justices," they were called. Marshall could not have relished his task.

On Adams' last day in office, March 3, the President was still appointing justices of the peace and his Federalist Congress was still hastily approving them. That night Marshall worked well after eight o'clock stamping commissions in his gloomy, deserted office. Finally, late in the evening, he had had enough. He departed for his boarding house, leaving a messy pile of papers on his desk, including twelve sealed but undelivered commissions. They would one day form the basis of an issue to plague him. Marshall, though, was through with being Secretary of State. Adams' administration was over. The Federalists were going out of Washington, leaving only Marshall as a powerful antagonist to Jefferson's expectation of keeping the Court insignificant.

☆

"There Is No Middle Ground"

The first law cases that came before Marshall as Chief Justice were not ones that were likely to arouse President Jefferson. They involved various technical decisions as to what particular laws meant, or how they applied in specific instances.

Trouble started in December, 1801. Charles Lee, a middle-aged Virginian and a Federalist attorney, came into court claiming that his client, William Marbury, had been granted a commission as Justice of the Peace by President Adams and that the commission had never been delivered. Lee demanded that the Court order the new Secretary of State, James Madison, to give Marbury his commission.

Charles Lee must have known that he was putting the Court in the worst possible position. Suppose they did order Madison to hand over the commission. How could they make him comply? The Court, unlike the President, did not command an armed force and, unlike Congress, could not withhold appropriations from Government departments of which it disapproved. If Marshall and the others dismissed the case, they would be admitting that the Court was powerless to enforce the law. If they gave Madison a chance to disobey them—which he was certain to do—they would all look like fools.

Marshall, eager to be a vigorous Chief Justice, was especially concerned with the matter. When a court sends an executive officer of the Government or of a private group an order demanding that the executive carry out some function of his office, that is called a "mandamus." Although Marshall knew that Jefferson had already spoken against Marbury's appointment, he sent Madison a bold message. Show cause, it said, why a mandamus should not be sent to you, making you deliver Marbury's commission.

Then Marshall commanded the clerk to docket the case—that is, put it on the calendar, to be heard at the Court's next term in June. Marshall, ready for the scrap, must have tingled with excitement as he watched the Court clerk pushing his scratchy quill pen over the yellow paper of the Court books, writing "Marbury v. Madison." If a fire was crackling that day in the courtroom fireplace, its flames were no hotter than Thomas Jefferson's anger would be when he heard the news.

The news soon electrified all of Washington. "High hand!" screamed the pro-Republican press. "Grounds for impeachment," suggested some outraged politicians. "Send the Judges back on circuit duty and keep them out of mischief," suggested others.

Spurred on by messages from the President, the Senate debated what to do about the judiciary. As was customary in those days, though unthinkable today, Marshall doubtless came and watched from the visitors' gallery at the back of the semicircular chamber, hearing the angry voice of Senator Jackson of Georgia refer to "their [the Court's] attack on the Secretary of State."

Senator Breckenridge of Kentucky formally proposed that at least the Judiciary Reform Act of the previous year could be repealed. The Supreme Court justices would then have to go back on circuit duty and the country could save the money paid the sixteen new circuit judges, as their posts could be eliminated.

Senator Breckenridge was soon challenged by an old veteran of the Revolution, Gouverneur Morris of New York, whose thoughts echoed Marshall's own. Senator Morris rose, flush-faced, and balanced himself awkwardly, handicapped by his wooden leg.

"What will be the effect of the desired repeal?" he shouted. "Will it not be a declaration to the remaining judges that they hold their offices subject to your will and pleasure?" A threat to destroy the Constitution, Morris termed the proposal, since the Constitution provided that Federal judges "shall hold their office during good behavior [i.e., for life] and receive . . . a compensation, which shall not be diminished during their continuance in office." The Constitution, Morris insisted, thus intended to make the justices independent enough to check the legislative and executive departments in any wanton invasion of our rights and, "to prevent an invasion of the Constitution by unconstitutional laws." Morris ended with the cry, "I declare to you, that if you lose this charter, never, no never, will you get another!"

Big, robust Senator Mason of Virginia took the floor. The justices, he said calmly, were to interpret and apply the laws, not to control the other departments of government.

The debate was repeated in the House of Representatives. Again and again, statesmen argued as to how powerful and how independent the Court should be. Finally, the legislature acted to intimidate the Court. The Judiciary reform bill of 1801 was repealed; the Supreme Court justices were sent back to circuit duty and the High Court was forbidden to meet for over a year. Congress was taking no chances that the circuit judges would rush to the Supreme Court demanding their appointments. The legislature simply abolished the Court's June and December meetings and decreed that the Court's next session was to be in the middle of the following February.

Marshall waited as the long months gradually passed. On the second Monday in February, 1803, he had the clerk call the case of *Marbury v. Madison.*

Then another problem arose: How could Lee prove that President Adams had actually signed Marbury's commission? Unless the commission had been signed it was not valid. Marshall knew, because the commission had been in his hands when he was Secretary of State, but as Chief Justice, he could not testify. That difficulty Lee would have to tackle.

When Lee led a frightened and self-effacing little clerk to the front of the room, Marshall recognized the man as Jacob Wagner, who worked in the office of Secretary of State. Wagner claimed that he had heard that Mr. Marbury's commission had been filled in, obviously by Marshall, and signed by the President.

Lee asked him where he got that information, but Wagner timidly refused to say.

Charles Lee then asked another clerk, Mr. Brent, to step forward, which he did with seemingly more poise and confidence than Wagner. He testified that various commissions had been made out for justices of the peace in the last moments of Mr. Adams' administration. He had carried them to the President's house and delivered them to Mr. Shaw, the President's aide, he said, and they had later been returned by messenger to the office of the Secretary of State.

Was Marbury's commission among the others? Lee asked.

Brent was almost certain it was.

Nobody in the room knew for sure, other than Marshall, and he must have been aware of the drollness of the situation as Lee attempted to prove to him what had happened in his own office only nine months before.

What became of the commissions? Lee persisted.

Brent said he didn't know.

Were they in the office?

Not to his knowledge. He hadn't seen them, Brent said.

Charles Lee tried once more. He hailed Attorney General Levi Lincoln into court. Crafty Mr. Lincoln had been in politics a long time. During the opening weeks of Jefferson's administration, he had been Secretary of State, and now he was Attorney General, the Government's principal legal officer.

Lee asked whether Mr. Lincoln would testify as to the existence of the commission and what had become of it. Levi Lincoln said he wasn't sure it was proper for him to answer the question. He had been in the Secretary of State's office only briefly and besides, he wasn't sure he should testify to facts that came to his knowledge in that office.

Would the Court, he inquired, have the questions put in writing? He wanted, he explained, to weigh his obligations—to ascertain his duty to President Jefferson and his duty to the Court and the law.

Later, in his decision, Marshall reprimanded Lincoln, maintaining that "The government of the United States has been emphatically termed a government of laws, and not of men." Heads of government departments are, he made clear then, obligated to obey the laws of their country. At that moment, though, all Marshall said was, "There is nothing confidential required to be disclosed. It is a fact which all the world has a right to know." What had happened to the commissions?

Levi Lincoln hedged. There were a considerable number of commissions for justice of the peace in the office when the Republicans took office, he admitted. But he refused to say that he had seen Marbury's.

With nothing accomplished, the Court adjourned until the next day, and it was then that Lee produced his crucial witness. James Marshall, the Chief Justice's younger brother, came to Lee's assistance. James had been in the office of the Secretary of State and had seen the signed and sealed but undelivered documents. After hearing what James had to say, the Court felt compelled to accept the existence of Marbury's commission and to decide what action to take.

Lee was allowed to argue his case. The Court should issue the mandamus, he maintained. His client was entitled to his commission, and the Court had the right to issue a mandamus to Madison because Section 13 of the Judiciary Act of 1789 gave the Court that right. The act said that the Supreme Court could issue writs of mandamus to persons holding office under the authority of the United States. By "writ" he meant a written message issued by the court, in behalf of the sovereign—a sovereign being a ruler or state with the power to govern.

Marshall asked if there was a reply, but no one came forward. No one spoke for the Government or for James Madison. Washington society fully expected that Marshall would issue the mandamus, and equally fully expected Madison not to obey it.

On February 24, Charles Lee returned to the little courtroom to learn what the six robed justices proposed to do. Marshall had written the decision and pronounced it from the bench for the Court.

He began by dividing the case into three questions. Has the applicant a right to his commission? If so, and his rights have been violated, do the laws of this country afford him any remedy? If they do afford him a remedy, is it a mandamus from *this* Court?

To the first question Marshall answered yes. William Marbury had already had his appointment when the Republicans took office, because the President had signed his commission. It could not be recalled.

As to question two, Marshall said, "The very essence of civil liberty certainly consists in the right of every individual to claim the protection of the laws, whenever he receives an injury. One of the first duties of government is to afford that protection." The Secretary of State, he declared, "cannot . . . sport away the vested rights of others." If he attempts to do so, he is answerable to the courts.

The Court, said Marshall, therefore had a right to hear the case. He agreed that a mandamus was in order.

Should the Supreme Court then issue the mandamus? As Marshall reminded Lee, according to the Constitution there are only two instances when the High Court rules on a case not first heard in the courts below: cases affecting representatives of foreign nations and cases in which a state is a party to the action. Neither description applied to the Marbury case.

It was true, Marshall conceded, that Section 13 of the Judiciary Act of 1789, passed by Congress, gave the High Court the additional power to issue writs to United States officials. It was on this basis that Lee had brought suit. Lee had, therefore, relied on the power of Congress to enlarge the Court's jurisdiction beyond the limits laid down in the Constitution. This Marshall could not uphold.

The departments of the United States government are limited in power, he declared, and "that those limits may not be mistaken, or forgotten, the constitution is written." A law contrary to the rules laid down in the Constitution "is void." Section 13 of the Judiciary Act of 1789, Marshall declared, was therefore void.

"It is," he explained, "emphatically the province and duty of the judicial department to say what the law is." He declared that "a legislative act contrary to the constitution is not law . . . It is a proposition too plain to be contested . . . there is no middle ground . . . the constitution is superior to any ordinary act of the legislature . . ."

The Court not only could, but had to, override such an act of Congress; for, as Marshall declared, he had taken an oath as Chief Justice to support the Constitution. Not to do so would be a crime.

Marbury, then, having sued in the wrong court, could not have his mandamus against Madison, and since his term of office was already more than half over, the "midnight Justice" felt forced to give up the claim to his commission.

President Jefferson couldn't attack this conclusion. As to ousting Marbury, he had his own way. But he had it solely because Section 13 of Judiciary Act of 1789, as passed by Congress, was unconstitutional and because the Court had the right to so rule.

Chief Justice Marshall, by his brilliant management of the whole situation, had won his own fight for the Court and the Constitution. He had majestically warned the members of the executive department that they must obey the law or be answerable to the courts. He had explained to the legislature, in a manner no longer to be refuted, that the Court could override any unconstitutional act; and he had, thereby, established the Court as the guardian of constitutional law. Since Marbury did not get a Court order issued against Madison, there was no way that the Secretary of State, the President or Congress could flout Marshall's decree. It stood, and became a precedent that is respected to this day.

An act of Congress contrary to the Constitution is not a law, and it is the Court's duty to nullify such an act. This principle has become a binding part of our American legal heritage and an important rampart for the protection of our rights and liberties. In proclaiming it, Marshall established the power and majesty of the Supreme Court.

Bibliography
Principal Sources, Case 1

BOOKS

Adams, John, *Works*. Boston. 1856.

Adams, Henry, *Life of Albert Gallatin*. Philadelphia. 1879.

Adams, John Quincy, *Memoirs*, Charles Francis Adams, ed. Philadelphia. 1874–77.

Beveridge, Albert J., *The Life of John Marshall.* Boston & New York. 1916.

Dillon, John F., compiler, *John Marshall, Life, Character and Judicial Services.* Chicago. 1903.

Elliot, Jonathan, compiler, *The Debates in the Several State Conventions on the Adoption of the Federal Constitution.* Washington. 1845.

Flanders, Henry, *The Lives and Times of the Chief Justices of the Supreme Court of the United States.* Philadelphia. 1855.

Jay, John, *The Correspondence and Public Papers of John Jay,* Henry P. Johnston, ed. New York. 1890.

Marshall, John, *An Autobiographical Sketch of John Marshall,* John Stokes Adams, ed. Michigan. 1937.

Smith, Margaret B., *The First Forty Years of Washington Society.* New York. 1906.

Warren, Charles, *The Supreme Court in United States History.* Boston. 1935.

UNITED STATES FEDERAL RECORDS

Annals, 7th Congress 1st Sess. 1802.

Marbury v. Madison, I Cranch 137 (1803).

Marshall, John, Original Letters to the District Commissioners. In the Archives Building, Washington, D.C.

Senate Document No. 62, 56 Congress 1st Sess. (1900). "Removal of the Seat of Government to the District of Columbia."

NEWSPAPERS

Aurora, General Advertiser, Philadelphia, Dec. 22, 30, 1801; Feb. 15, 1803.

Pennsylvania Journal, Nov. 14, 1787.

☆ CASE 2 ☆

McCulloch v. Maryland

The Court Affirms the Power of Congress

"This government . . . can exercise only the powers granted to it."

JOHN MARSHALL, 1819

THE TIMES
AND THE ISSUES

For a long time politicians who feared the effect of a strong federal government over the states demanded a narrow and rigid reading of the Constitution. Congress, they said, had no powers except those that were clearly stated. If the word corporation did not appear, then, they claimed, Congress could not incorporate a bank.

But the men who framed the Constitution realized that if it was to last, it had to be written in broad terms. How else could future problems, yet unknown, ever be solved?

Inevitably then, the question of the implied powers of Congress and the question of states' rights clashed in the famous battle over the Second United States Bank. The case that brought it to court, in 1819, was that of [Cashier James] *McCulloch v.* [the State of] *Maryland.*

☆

"Anyone with Enough Paper and a Printing Press Can Start a Bank"

On a September day in 1814, Alexander Dallas sat at his desk in his gracious Philadelphia home and wrote to Secretary of State James Monroe, "If I could be made serviceable to you in any way, I would gladly embrace the opportunity. . . ."

The letter was a gentle hint that Dallas, a wealthy attorney, would be willing to give up his large income and live on $5,000 a year if he could be Secretary of the Treasury. The calm words hid the deep anxiety that Dallas felt for his country.

The United States, then fighting its second war against Great Britain, was in such a state of financial chaos that the Government couldn't raise the funds to equip the Army. The war had started over Britain's unwillingness to recognize the rights of American merchant ships to trade with his Majesty's enemy, France. A worse danger to trade than the British, Dallas felt, was the disorderly state of the nation's currency.

Gold and silver coins were the only legal currency. But it was impossible to carry a bag of coins safely over the country's bad roads, so people frequently paid their debts and their taxes with printed bank notes.

Each fifty-dollar bank note was supposed to represent fifty dollars in gold or silver held in a banker's vault. Bankers, though, often printed many more notes than they could exchange for coin. Much of this paper couldn't be cashed or spent, at least not at its face value—and the United States Treasury, like many a private businessman, took a tragic loss.

The only remedy Dallas could think of was to start a United States bank. The bank could have branches in all the big cities, accept tax payments and lend the Government the money it needed in anticipation of tax collections. A Federal bank issuing notes to its depositors and shareholders would, besides, give the local banks

badly needed competition and make them watch what they were
doing.

For years Dallas had lobbied for such a bank. He pointed out
that President George Washington's Secretary of the Treasury,
Alexander Hamilton, had succeeded in getting Congress to charter
a bank for twenty years. Immediately, however, infuriated statesmen had insisted that "that bank was unconstitutional." The bank
was a corporation, they said, and nowhere did the Constitution give
Congress the power to launch a corporation. When the first bank's
charter ran out in 1811, Dallas had fought in vain to persuade the
legislature to renew it.

Recently, though, things had happened to convince Dallas that
he should start the fight again. First, George W. Campbell had
resigned as Secretary of the Treasury. When Congress had authorized him to borrow twenty-five million dollars, eleven and a half
million had been all the Secretary could scrape up from the country's financiers and moneylenders. Admitting that he had no idea
how the nation could carry on, Campbell had given up his post.

Then, only the previous month, President Madison had sent out
a proclamation ordering Congress into a special emergency session.
The President must be worried. The condition of the Treasury,
Dallas knew from financial contacts, could best be described as
nearly hopeless.

Dallas felt the lawmakers now might want to consider the idea of
a bank if it came from a Secretary of the Treasury. Of course, the
President would first have to cope with the fact that the seriousness
of the situation was perhaps not fully understood by all the senators
and representatives, since it was not fully grasped across the country.

One newspaper in Maine—then part of Massachusetts—printed
the President's summons to Congress along with the headline
"Rumors of Peace." These rumors seemed believable because
American ambassadors were in Ghent, Belgium, trying to arrange a
meeting with the English. But as the paper went to press, British
regulars, far from planning a peace, were landing on the banks of
the Potomac. After marching to the capital, they plundered offices
and hurled burning torches that set public buildings aflame. A sudden rain was all that saved the city.

When Dallas' letter arrived in Washington, the once-busy streets
were almost deserted. The roof of the Representatives' wing of the

Capitol was burned and caved in, and here and there a smaller building was in charred ruins.

The White House was unusable. The President had set up temporary quarters in a downtown office building. The Supreme Court met in the home of a clerk. The District Commissioners arranged to have the congressmen gather in the Patent Office Exhibit Hall.

On reaching the Exhibit Hall, congressmen were disgusted. The room was crowded, the air was hot and stale, and chairs were jammed close together. Each representative took a seat eyeing Speaker Cheves, who sat behind a table at the end of the hall facing the others. Thin-rimmed spectacles hugged Cheves' narrow face below his receding hair line, and except for his gavel, he might have resembled a schoolmaster calling on his boys to recite.

The assembly received the President's special message at noon on the twentieth of September. The delivery boy carrying the message was escorted by the doorkeeper to the Speaker's table, and a clerk standing by the table read Mr. Madison's words to the listening congressmen.

"Notwithstanding the early days which had been fixed for your session, I was induced to call you together still sooner," the President began. He went on to explain that this was a war crisis.

No word had been received from the United States ambassadors who were attempting to negotiate a peace with the British. Hostilities, in fact, continued more violently than ever.

The President then quickly came to his point. The moneys received into the Treasury during the past nine months had not equaled disbursements, he informed Congress. "The war," he said, "will render it necessary that large sums be provided . . . on a scale commensurate with the extent and the character which the war has assumed. This . . . Congress will be urged to take up without delay. . . . Our enemy . . . is aiming . . . a deadly blow at . . . our national existence."

A concerned silence engulfed the listening audience. How were they to raise still more funds?

Taxes could be raised, but with trade under a blockade and financial conditions wretched in many parts of the country, not enough would be gained.

The House assigned the problem to the Ways and Means Committee with instructions to form a plan of action. September slipped away. The warm weather subsided and still the committee, led by Chairman J. W. Eppes of Virginia, did not agree as to what should be done. Congressmen worried about the country's soldiers facing the coming winter. Losses could be terrible if appropriations weren't raised at once for warm clothing and blankets. And how could fresh recruits be mobilized unless money was found to pay and equip them? Unless the nation could display great strength, there was little hope that the ambassadors at Ghent could achieve a settlement.

Congressman John C. Calhoun of South Carolina expressed these fears when he stood on the floor of the House, shouting, "If ever a body of men held the destinies of a country in its hands [it is this body] . . . We have not a moment to lose." But his impatience did not produce a solution.

Meanwhile, President Madison, working in his little temporary study, saw Dallas' letter. Secretary of State James Monroe brought it to the President's attention. It must have brought a smile to his eyes. President Madison was well aware why Dallas, with an income of more than twenty thousand a year in fees, was thus hinting that he would give up his fine legal practice and live in a Washington boarding house. But from the President's point of view, the bank scheme was exactly what was needed. The Government certainly could not go on begging loans from a few rich and unwilling businessmen. In addition, Mr. Madison knew that Dallas' plan had great value beyond the present crisis. A bank that could issue a usable paper currency would be a vital institution in peacetime for a more prosperous America. It was a wartime necessity.

As things stood, a hundred-dollar bank note from a traveler's home town wouldn't buy fifty cents' worth of postage in a neighboring state if his bank was unknown, for, as one newspaper put it, "Anyone with enough paper and a printing press can start a bank."

The President turned his attention to the difficulties of getting Congress to accept the Dallas proposal. Many of the lawmakers, led by J. W. Eppes, the Ways and Means Committee chairman, still thought that the Constitution did not give them the legal right to incorporate a bank. President Madison understood their arguments. He had once agreed with them, but now that three years without a Federal bank had ended in financial havoc, he gratefully recalled how Hamilton had argued. The Constitution gave Congress the right to make what laws were necessary for carrying out the Government's duties. Therefore, Hamilton said, Congress had the *implied* power to start a bank because a bank could be used to assist Congress in paying debts, collecting taxes and regulating the currency.

The President no longer doubted that his administration needed to regulate the currency. He wrote the Senate a message strongly expressing his wish that they confirm Alexander Dallas as Secretary of the Treasury.

The strongest opposition to Dallas came from Abner Lacock, a Senator from Dallas' own state of Pennsylvania. Lacock branded Dallas a mouthpiece for the money interests. For days he discussed Dallas with all of his colleagues, but the other senators' arguments must have influenced the Pennsylvanian, for at last Lacock called on President Madison's private secretary, to say, "Tell 'Doctor' Madison we are now willing to submit to his Philadelphia lawyer for the head of the Treasury. The public patient is so sick that we must swallow anything the doctor prescribes."

That meant that the Senate would cooperate in the plan for a bank; Dallas' beliefs were well known to them. But what action the House of Representatives would take still remained a mystery. Dallas tackled the problem of getting Congressional approval for his bank as soon as he arrived in Washington on October 14. He arranged a private meeting with Congressman John C. Calhoun, the tall, dark-haired, and dynamic chairman of the House Currency Committee.

If Calhoun came to the interview expecting to meet a hard man of figures, he was surprised. Dallas, reared in Jamaica, had a sensitive face framed by soft, curly hair parted on the side. All the tropical warmth of his West Indian island home seemed to burst forth in his excited arguments for his cherished scheme of establishing a new Federal bank. Calhoun left promising his support; and Dallas, delighted, wrote Congress a message recommending a Federal bank.

However, the end of January found the weary congressmen still debating the question. Calhoun had slowed up debate by writing his own bank bill, which competed with Dallas' proposal and split the bank supporters apart. Not until after the Dallas measure had been defeated by a tie vote did Calhoun realize he was jeopardizing the country by dividing the House.

Then on February 14 a messenger arrived on horseback from New York harbor bearing good news. The proposed peace treaty had been signed at Ghent on Christmas Eve.

After the Senate ratified the treaty on February 17 the congressmen were as hopelessly gripped by inaction as if they had been frozen into blocks of ice by the weather.

There was still no money to run the Government or pay the war debts. The economic plight of the country still would have to be righted, but it would all have to wait. The congressmen were so relieved to hear that the war was over that they could not be contained in dreary, over-crowded Washington. They wanted to be home attending to their families and their own affairs. They adjourned in March.

As more time elapsed, farmers and businessmen suffered for lack of a reliable currency and the Government was desperate for fresh credit. Dallas eagerly awaited the 1816 session of Congress, and fortunately, its work went more smoothly. Now, his opposition to Dallas' bank bill broken by his own conscience, Calhoun actually helped to fight for it.

With his assistance the congressmen managed to pass the bank bill in April, 1816. In its final form it was much as Dallas had planned it, except that it was to pay, not lend, the Government a million and a half dollars. With joy and relief, one congressman explained, "It will usher in a new day replete with benefits for the nation." If the majority agreed, it was because no one could foresee the dreadful scene that would take place in America only two years later.

The enemies of the bank bill were not silenced and Dame Nature was to become their strongest supporter. The spring of 1818 brought with it a drought. Pasture lands scorched brown, corn and tobacco leaves withered and wheat failed to germinate. Ruined farmers couldn't meet their bank payments, and the sheriff auctioned off their property.

Shopkeepers felt the sting when the farmers couldn't come to buy. Meanwhile, the nation's wharfs bustled with stevedores unloading crates of European goods that the shopkeepers were committed to accept. The frantic merchants canceled their orders for home-made products, and American industry was in trouble.

The confused, unhappy people blamed the new national Bank. The Bank at first had been willing to give a man a loan and allow him to make his interest payments with local bank notes. Now, in a bad year, when people were desperate for money, the wretched managers were cutting off credit. Doggedly, they refused to renew old loans. By August, they would be refusing to accept the notes of other banks. Moreover, since bank notes promised that the issuer was holding so much gold coin, the managers of the United States Bank were confronting local bankers with their old notes and demanding their coin. As a result, banks closed and some failed.

Actually, United States Bank managers had already made more loans and accepted more promissory notes than they could carry and still meet their obligation to the Federal government. They were frightened by the state of their own affairs. But all the debtors understood was that their local bankers, having to find gold to feed the Federal vulture, were doing the inevitable—hounding a man for the money he owed, foreclosing his mortgage and seizing his home. Encouraged by their local bankers, borrowers were convinced that the United States Bank was the demon. State legislators laid plans to strangle this "monster" that was gobbling up their constituents' property. The next episode in the war against the Bank took place in Maryland.

☆

"The Power to Tax Involves the Power to Destroy"

Strangely, the threatening assault on the United States Bank did not in the least perturb James McCulloch, cashier of the Baltimore branch of the Bank.

McCulloch was a popular man. When he walked down the cobbled streets of Baltimore, he was warmly greeted. The tradesmen who kept store on the ground floor of their two- and three-story brick buildings liked him and found him a good customer. As yet nobody knew that while working in the second floor apartment, which housed the Baltimore branch office, James McCulloch was lending himself money at no interest and simply renewing his own pledges when they came due.

While McCulloch was thus getting rich, the Maryland legislature was working to appease the angry clamor of Maryland bankers who resented the Federal institution. The statesmen passed a law designed to make it impossible for the United States Bank to compete with local firms. The United States Bank was either to pay the huge annual tax of fifteen thousand dollars or issue all of its notes on paper bearing a Maryland tax stamp. McCulloch's only reaction was, "How dare they!" He was not going to pay a tax.

Then, late in the spring of 1818, McCulloch had an impressive visitor. George Williams, a director of the Bank's main office in Philadelphia, called on the Baltimore branch cashier. Williams had a nearby residence and had come home for a stay. He explained that he needed money.

McCulloch issued the director United States Bank notes on paper that did not bear the Maryland tax stamp. Williams spent the notes and this unstamped paper circulated around Baltimore until an informer named John James reported the episode to the Maryland authorities.

Hence, on the morning of May 8, McCulloch found himself standing before a judge in the little Baltimore County courtroom. McCulloch insisted that Maryland couldn't tax a Federal bank; that was tantamount to taxing the Federal government. A mere state couldn't tax the Federal government. But the judge ruled against the cashier and ordered him to pay a fine of one hundred dollars. McCulloch answered that he would appeal the case to the higher courts.

On hearing the story, the administration in Washington was immediately aroused. The Maryland law, officials said, was an open attempt to tax their bank out of existence by making its notes expensive. Marylanders were trying to override an act of Congress. The bank issue, they saw, involved more than the implied powers of Congress to start a bank. Now it also involved another question. Which was to be supreme, the states or the Federal government?

President Monroe's administration at once directed the Attorney General to fight McCulloch's case. But in spite of everything Attorney General William Wirt could say, the Maryland Court of Appeals upheld the county judge. Wirt then took the case of *McCulloch v. Maryland* to the Supreme Court of the United States.

Maryland Attorney General Luther Martin prepared to counter Wirt's attack. He would demolish the Bank, he stated, by persuading the Supreme Court to declare the law creating the Bank unconstitutional.

At the time, the Supreme Court justices were meeting in the Capitol basement, which had been repaired after the war. A small semicircular courtroom had been constructed for their use, and it was there that they assembled on February 22, 1819, to hear arguments on two issues: Did Congress have the implied power to charter a bank? If so, could the State of Maryland control it by taxation?

With the country in a state of financial panic, popular concern over the Bank issue was evident. Spectators jammed into every available seat in the little courtroom. Chief Justice Marshall himself was awed by the significance of the case. In his opening remarks to the Court, he stated, "The conflicting powers of the government of the Union and of its members, as marked in the Constitution, are to be discussed; and an opinion given, which may essentially influence the great operations of the government. No tribunal can approach such a question without a deep sense of its importance, and the awful responsibility involved in its decision."

Because of the seriousness of the issue, the Court waived its own rule that permitted only two counsels to argue for each party. Six attorneys, three for each side, argued for nine days.

Daniel Webster agreed to speak first, for the Bank. He appeared grandly dressed in tight breeches and a cutaway coat with brass buttons.

Three decades, he pointed out, had now elapsed since Hamilton first debated the constitutionality of the Bank with Thomas Jefferson and then with the legislature. At that time, President Washington had solved the problem by siding with Hamilton. Webster's colleague in the case, William Pinkney, explained the point, saying, "The question has been long since settled by decision of the most revered authority. . . . A legislative construction, in a doubtful case, persevered in for a course of years, ought to be binding upon the court."

Webster went on to review Hamilton's argument that Congress had implied powers to make any laws that were necessary for carrying out the legislative functions. Webster said the Bank was necessary, and that if Maryland could tax it, she could destroy it. It was unthinkable to give one state that much power over the Federal government, he concluded.

Webster was still young. Luther Martin, Attorney General of Maryland, was seventy-five years old. He rose to tell his youthful opponent that if the states had ever expected that the Congress of the United States was to assume powers not specifically stated in the Constitution, the document would never have been ratified. The word "bank" did not appear in the Constitution. Besides, Maryland could tax anything within her borders and the Federal government couldn't stop her. The Constitution, Martin said, was a compact between the states and they alone remained supreme. Martin then quoted Marshall's own words at the Virginia Convention in 1789 promising that the United States government would be limited in power. An associate justice, Joseph Story, noticed that the listening Chief Justice turned pale.

After that, the other attorneys were heard and the case dragged to its conclusion. Then it took Marshall only three days to write the opinion of a unanimous court. On March 6, the Chief Justice delivered his historic decision from the bench.

Marshall recognized the truth of Webster's statement that the friends of the Bank could claim it had been endorsed by several Congresses. Legal tradition is usually a powerful argument at the bar, but this time it was not enough. Marshall felt it necessary to examine the position taken by Luther Martin. This he proceeded to do.

To begin with, the counsel for the State of Maryland, Marshall said, considered the Constitution not as coming from the people but rather as an act of independent states. Before going further with his decision, Marshall wanted to clear up that point. His ire was up.

The men who framed the Constitution were indeed selected by the state legislatures. "But," Marshall said, "the instrument, when it came from their hands, was a mere proposal. . . . It was reported to the then existing congress of the United States . . . [and] submitted to a convention of delegates, chosen in each State by the people." The people acted upon it, he explained.

The states, Marshall explained, had agreed to accept the will of the people. They arranged for the chosen delegates to meet in convention. "The government of the Union, then," said the Chief Justice, "is, emphatically, and truly, a government of the people"— which bound the state sovereignties.

Luther Martin had charged that Marshall had promised the Virginia Convention that the new government of the United States would be limited in power. Said Marshall, "This government . . . can exercise only the powers granted to it." Therefore, the problem was to interpret the extent of those powers.

Luther Martin claimed that the powers of Congress were not supreme over the states. Marshall said, "The Government of the Union, though limited in its powers, *is* supreme. . . . It is the government of all; . . . it represents all, and acts for all." In other words, that government, which was elected by the people of all the states, had to be the supreme government in the land. Therefore, no state could control or obstruct the actions of the people of the Union or their law makers.

"The nation, on those subjects on which it can act must necessarily bind its component parts," Marshall said. He referred to the Constitution: "This Constitution, and the laws of the United States, which shall be made in pursuance thereof . . . shall be the supreme law of the land."

"We, the people," Marshall said, "had so decided." If Congress could start a bank, Maryland could not control it by taxation.

But had the Government exceeded its rights, as Maryland claimed, when it chartered the Bank? Had it unjustly seized and usurped additional powers? Marshall admitted that among the enumerated powers of Congress we do not find that of establishing a bank or creating a corporation.

"The power of creating a corporation," Marshall explained, "is not . . . a great . . . independent power . . . but a means by which other objects are accomplished."

He pictured a bank aiding in the collection of taxes and in borrowing money to supply armies and navies in time of war.

The Constitution, he pointed out, gave Congress the right to make all laws necessary for putting the Government's powers into action. He gave a vivid example. The words of the Constitution on the subject of a post office say only this: "Congress shall have the power . . . to establish Post Offices and Post Roads." From this phrase, Marshall explained, comes the obvious and implied power and duty to carry the mail from one Post Office to another, and to send out officers to stalk, ambush and bring to justice those who rob the mails. Such measures, he said, are necessary to the functions of government and so were intended by the words of the Constitution.

The Bank, then, was constitutional, and Maryland could not tax it, "for the power to tax involves the power to destroy," Marshall

said, and "the power to destroy may defeat the power to create."
The states could not thus dictate what means Congress should use
to achieve its ends. The Constitution said that power was to rest
with Congress. So long as Congress picked appropriate means to
carry out its functions, and so long as those means were within the
spirit of the Constitution, they were constitutional, Marshall explained.

Here Marshall asserted the power of the Court to overturn a law
passed by one of the states. Here, too, Marshall turned into law
the principle of the implied powers of Congress claimed earlier by
George Washington and Alexander Hamilton. And in so doing he
breathed into the Constitution of the United States a flexibility that
gives hope of perpetual life.

As the years rolled by, Congress set up many corporations to
deal with crises similar to those experienced by the people of
1819. To guard against worthless bank notes and so regulate the
currency, Congress in 1912 set up the Federal Reserve System.

To protect the public from unsound banks, the Congress in 1933
launched the Federal Deposit Insurance Corporation, to which almost all banks belong. Even if a member bank goes into bankruptcy, a man can get his savings. The F.D.I.C. pays him.

Establishing corporations is not the only use to which Congress
has put its implied powers. For example, it established unemploy-
ment insurance and old age insurance. These, though challenged,
have been held constitutional by the Court because Congress can
collect taxes to provide for the general welfare of the United
States.

Congress has also developed a licensing system to allocate the
use of radio and television channels. All this and much, much more
was made possible on the March morning in 1819 when Marshall
ruled on the case of *McCulloch v. Maryland.*

McCulloch's dishonesty was eventually discovered and he was
put out of the Bank. President Jackson later withdrew all Government funds, causing the collapse of the Second United States Bank.
Abraham Lincoln's armies had to fight for the principle that the
Union was greater than its parts because the government of the
Union alone represents all the people. Nevertheless, one great question had been answered by the McCulloch-Maryland case. It established that Congress had the implied power to choose any means
not prohibited by law to carry out its legal goals. Without this
power, the United States government could not provide for the

American people's needs. Through the ravages of many times and many problems, it has been the use of this implied power by Congress that has preserved the nation. And so Marshall intended.

Bibliography
Principal Sources, Case 2

BOOKS

Adams, Henry, *The Life of Albert Gallatin*. Philadelphia. 1879.

Bryan, Wilhelmus Bogart, *A History of the National Capitol*. New York. 1914–16.

Catterall, Ralph, *The Second Bank of the United States*. Chicago. 1903.

Channing, Edward, *A History of the United States*. New York. 1905–1925.

Curtis, George Ticknor, *Life of Webster*. New York. 1870

Ingersoll, Charles J., *History of the Second War Between the United States of America and Great Britain*. Philadelphia. 1852.

Hamilton, Alexander, Madison, James, and Jay, John, *The Federalist*. Jacob E. Cooke, ed., Middletown, Conn. 1961.

Hart, Albert B., *Documents Relative to the Bank Controversy*. New York. 1895.

Harvey, Peter, *Reminiscences and Anecdotes of Daniel Webster*. Boston, 1877.

Madison, James, *Letter and Other Writings, published by Order of Congress*. Washington. 1856.

Webster, Daniel, *The Works of Daniel Webster*. Boston. 1853.

Webster, Daniel, *The Private Correspondence of Daniel Webster*. Fletcher Webster, ed. Boston. 1857.

UNITED STATES FEDERAL RECORDS

Annals of Congress, Years 1814, 1815, and 1816.

McCulloch v. Maryland, 4 Wheaton 316 (1819).

NEWSPAPERS

American Advocate, Maine, August 20, 1814.

National Intelligencer, Washington, August 9, 1814.

Savannah Republican, Georgia, August 18, 20, 1814.

☆ CASE 3 ☆

Trustees of Dartmouth College v. Woodward

The Court Rules that a State Must Keep Its Agreements

"No State shall . . . pass any . . . law impairing the obligation of contracts."

THE CONSTITUTION OF THE UNITED STATES

THE TIMES
AND THE ISSUES

American businessmen envisioned a glorious future after the War of 1812. During the war they had been unable to get manufactured goods from abroad and so had built their own mills and factories. Now they wanted more industries.

Adventurous investors, when launching an enterprise, however, needed a charter of incorporation from their state. Only the charter gave them the power to run a corporation. The dispute in the Dartmouth College case raged over whether this charter, once granted, was a contract. Should it not be a reliable agreement, free of the constant danger of being revoked by the legislature? Shouldn't it be safe from the rise and fall of political parties? If not, who but the reckless would finance a business? America's whole economic future depended on this decision.

Strangely, the quarrel that began the case involved college boys and their elders, far from the centers of commerce. Among the pines and the maples of rural New Hampshire, in a clearing near the little town of Hanover, stood the red brick buildings of Dartmouth College. That is where the next story begins.

☆

―――――――

―――――――

"They Have Violated the Charter!"

A student stepped gingerly into the barren office of President John Wheelock of Dartmouth. Earlier, Wheelock had been a Lieutenant Colonel in the Continental Army and now, in the year 1815, he fought hard to be in command of every situation. Behind his study desk Wheelock sat erect, as if he were still in uniform. He wore, instead, a dun-colored coat, knee breeches and white stockings. His smooth brown hair was parted in the middle and tied tightly in back.

If Wheelock had any liking for the student he did not show it.

He listened icily as the youth delivered a message and then stood awkwardly wondering what to do.

"Well," Wheelock barked, "will you go now?"

Obligingly, the youth fled to the semicircle of green in front of Dartmouth Hall, where he met his friends—husky, unaffected boys from the neighboring farming communities. Wheelock considered them louts. They thought him a tyrant and a bore.

The president's theology class met in the two-story red brick Hall on Saturday afternoons, and the boys sat on hard wooden seats and gave him their strict attention. They dared do nothing else. They enjoyed discussing religion, but Wheelock would let no one say anything except what was written in the textbook. He made everything dull, the boys complained, but the one word "dismissed."

The youths were not alone in their complaints. Local farmers grumbled, too. Wheelock had lent various neighbors money at a high rate of interest and then was quick to foreclose their property. He also meddled in their local church affairs, imposing his will on everybody.

All this the students knew, and they guessed that there was trouble brewing from another quarter, as well. Wheelock had told one of them that the Dartmouth trustees were harsh. The boys thought Wheelock should have shown more respect. Wheelock, they decided, should remember who the trustees were.

There was Stephen J. Jacob, a poet; Timothy Farrar, an ex-associate judge of the State Supreme Court; and Elijah Paine, who was also a judge. Thomas W. Thompson was a United States senator and Charles Marsh was a member of Congress. There were three others, with the right to put Reverend before their names.

The youths took pride in being part of the college along with men like these. Impressive, too, was the scholarship of Professor Shurtleff, a large and clever man who taught literature, and the students warmed to the friendliness of Professor Adams, who taught philosophy. The boys felt that these professors, the alumni, and the student body, together with the trustees, were Dartmouth!

When the Dartmouth trustees dined together in a private home in Hanover, their comments showed they were straining their patience over the effect Wheelock was having on the college. How dared he be outraged when they refused to become embroiled in his village quarrels, and when would he act on their request that he provide more educational opportunities for the Indians?

Marsh, Paine and Thompson had another criticism. His class in wills was poorly taught, but he would do nothing to improve the course. He considered every suggestion an affront.

Soon the trustees had more to complain about. Unsigned pamphlets appeared in the shops of Hanover. Students bought them, carried them back to their dormitories and examined every word of the small print.

The pamphlets accused the trustees of using college funds improperly to finance village preaching, of being extravagant, and of improperly interfering with teaching methods. A stranger walking across the commons would have heard over and over the words "Wheelock" . . . "pamphlet" . . . "libel." There was no question in the boys' minds as to who had written the libelous words. Their sense of loyalty was outraged.

Judge Paine and Senator Thompson went to the printer's shop and demanded to know who had ordered the pamphlet published. The printer put the original manuscript on a table for them to look at, and the handwriting was Wheelock's. Exasperated, the trustees called a meeting and discharged Wheelock. In his place they elected Francis Brown president. However, if they thought that was to be the end of their troubles, they were mistaken.

Wheelock, they learned, had repeated his complaints to the state legislature. It was easy to imagine him in Concord, holding his old, three-cornered hat in his hand and pretending to be humble.

He entreated "the Honorable Body" to consider the state of the college. "They have violated the charter," he said, "and taken away the rights it expressly invests in the president." Then he repeated what he had said in the pamphlets. School funds were being used improperly to finance preaching for the villagers. There was much extravagance.

The trustees were known to be Federalists. Governor Plumer and the majority of the legislators listening to Wheelock were Jeffersonian Republicans like Wheelock. The lawmakers, therefore, quickly believed that the trustees must be power-hungry autocrats mismanaging the college.

That spring the boys on campus and around the study halls had more to talk about. Portly gentlemen in frock coats arrived from Concord to investigate the college. William Woodward, the college secretary, opened the books for their inspection. Then they sat around a long table in a Hanover residence holding their quill pens and questioning the trustees.

It may have been Marsh or Paine among the trustees who pointed out that actually Wheelock had agreed to their plans to provide preaching for the townsfolk. The townsfolk had raised the money to build the Meeting House and the college also used it.

All the trustees admitted that Wheelock's father—the great Eleazar Wheelock, founder of Dartmouth—had willed his son the presidency of the college. But, they explained, they had too long suffered Wheelock's obstinacy on that account. As trustees they had obligations toward the students. Wheelock's attitudes toward the boys and toward the farmers were hurting the school. As far as extravagance was concerned, they said, the investigators could see for themselves. There was none.

The investigators seemed impressed. They took their report back to the State House. But before they had time to get all their findings printed, the legislature acted. On June 27, 1816, the lawmakers deprived the Dartmouth trustees of their charter.

Graduation day found the boys gathering in front of Dartmouth Hall to form a procession to the Meeting House. Some were in knee breeches, some in the new full-length trousers. There was no trace of the gay excitement that usually went with seeing Seniors get diplomas. The boys and their friends all knew that by losing their charter the trustees had lost the right to run the college. The legislature had ordered Dartmouth College discontinued and planned later to replace her. They had amended the charter to form a state university, which would operate under the governor and a board of overseers.

Already one of the overseers had asked Professor Shurtleff for the key to the library. The new university board wanted to have a meeting, the overseer explained. Shurtleff referred him to President Brown, who said he did not have the authority to give up the key.

Now, Thompson and Marsh, Farrar and Paine and the others were seated in Brown's parlor, debating what to do.

How could the legislature revoke their charter? A charter was a contract. This was confiscation of property!

Judge Paine agreed with the others. "If we are to resort to the courts to obtain our rights, I think the sooner it is done the better," he said.

The other trustees looked at each other. They knew they hadn't the money to pay for a court case. Nevertheless, with nothing to fight with but their courage, they sent the governor a message:

"Resolved that we, the Trustees of Dartmouth College, do not accept the provisions of an act of the Legislature of New Hampshire passed June 27, 1816, and do hereby expressly refuse to act under the same."

The trustees then filed out of the cottage and walked slowly down Brown's hill watching the procession. The seriousness of their own words must have weighed heavily on their minds. They were defying the state government. What would happen to them now they did not know.

Dignitaries, both military and civilian, lined the pews of the white-walled Meeting House. Hymns were sung and speeches delivered in Latin for the benefit of the graduates. As heads bent in prayer, more than one trustee must have asked the Lord to soften the hearts of the legislature.

Government retaliation came—right after Christmas. Governor Plumer made sharp remarks about teaching youths to resist the law. He pushed through the legislature a bill levying a five hundred dollar fine on anyone acting as professor or trustee of Dartmouth College.

The trustees answered that depriving them of their charter was not law, but lawlessness. They were going to continue the school, but their secretary, William Woodward, had other ideas. He joined the university board, taking with him the Dartmouth College seal and records.

Then President Brown was offered a better job at another school. The faculty at Dartmouth was small. If Brown left, trying to continue seemed useless. There were many students and villagers who thought it was equally senseless for the trustees to continue to hope to get the college charter back if they hadn't the necessary funds for a court action.

Professor Adams discussed the problem with his friend and house guest, John Wheeler. Wheeler was a hard-working farmer and a muscular woodsman. Having learned his own lessons at night, by candlelight, he had a great respect for education, and being a great admirer of Adams, he listened sympathetically to the professor's troubles.

The college might be unable to go on. They lacked the money for a court case, the professor explained. After Wheeler put his savings at the school's disposal, Brown decided against leaving Dartmouth in her time of trouble. And the trustees took their case to court. Their principal attorney was one of their own alumni, Daniel Webster.

Webster and two colleagues appeared before the three judges of the New Hampshire Superior Court to demand the return of the college seal and records and above all the college charter.

"Declare the act of the legislature void," they pleaded. They insisted that since it had acted to deprive the trustees of their charter rights and property, it had violated a contract.

Judge William Richardson, the chief justice, said he did not think the trustees had any case whatever. Dartmouth did not exist for their benefit. It was not their personal property, even if they had given money to support it. The founders of the college wanted to benefit the youth of New Hampshire, and Dartmouth College was therefore intended as a public service. He saw no reason, then, why the elected representatives of the people should not change the college to a state university under different management.

The state, he said, granted charters, and so the state could withdraw them. The court did not concede that the charter was a contract. Richardson, speaking for himself and the two other judges, refused to nullify the act of the legislature and refused to order Mr. Woodward to return the college seal and records.

Furious, Daniel Webster announced that he would take the case to the United States Supreme Court. When the New Hampshire legislators learned of the Superior Court's decision they did not take Webster's threat seriously. They did not think the Supreme Court would even agree to hear Webster, and they were certain that he could not win. As far as they were concerned, the issue was settled. And now that both the legislature and the courts had acted, pew holders in the Meeting House were divided in their sympathies. Some still supported the college, others spoke up for their state officials.

The night before the spring term was to start, President Brown heard the crash of breaking glass in the area of Dartmouth Hall. As he hurried across the campus he was joined by Adams and Shurtleff and then by a gang of students.

Townspeople, they found, were hoisting Indians into the building through broken windows. The Indians cracked open the doors and then the townsmen installed new locks. They were hired by the university overseers, they explained, to take possession of the college and its library.

The students and professors must have made frantic preparations that night, for the next day in Hanover, when a Senior blew a signal on a horn, all the one hundred and thirty Dartmouth college boys filed into a hall over the hat shop. There they began their semester's work.

Many of the college boys were already living in private homes. Others moved into a two-story building near Shurtleff's cottage and used it for a dormitory. For books, the boys had to rely on a library owned by a student club called the Social Friends. Classes met in the professors' homes.

The overseers continued to use Dartmouth Hall for their "own" university students. "Wheelock men," the college boys called them, for Wheelock had been named president of the University by the overseers. Before he died, in April, he had instilled in his new students his own malice against the ousted college.

The new university men tried to break into the Social Friends' library and steal the college boys' books. They surrounded the meeting hall at graduation and tried to stop the college commencement exercises. They were intent on smashing what was left of Dartmouth College before her Trustees could raise enough additional funds to take the case to the Supreme Court. The college boys did gang up to chase off the "Wheelock men," but local law was not with them and it was a dangerous business.

☆

"If the Constitution Be Not Altogether Waste Paper . . . !"

In March of 1818, when Daniel Webster finally managed to bring the Dartmouth College case before the Supreme Court, the overseers showed little concern. Webster had not yet argued the Bank case and was not as yet the famous statesman-orator that he later became.

Besides, as the overseers reminded everyone, Associate Justice Joseph Story was a personal friend of Governor Plumer. Story, they recalled, had even been offered a post at the university. True, he had turned it down, but he gave no indication that he was out of sympathy with the new arrangement.

Joseph Story, in addition, was a Republican, as was another new justice, Gabriel Duval. President Madison, by adding these two men to Jefferson's earlier appointments of Johnson, Livingston and Todd, had made the now seven-man bench overwhelmingly Republican. Of the old Federalists, only John Marshall and Bushrod Washington remained. Story, the overseers were sure, would convince the other Republican judges of the worthiness of their cause. They had nothing to fear.

There are those who say that Webster himself had very little hope of success. If so, he did not show it when he rose before the bench, his strong face solemn above his frilled shirt and his blue cutaway coat.

He started by explaining that Dartmouth had been a private charity for half a century; that her charter was granted by George III, making her a corporation; that, as far as the trustees were concerned, the charter was a contract. In return for the grant of corporate powers, the trustees had agreed to conduct a college.

They had used their assets and reputations for the good of the school. They would not have done so had they expected that the state could later take away their control over the property.

"That all property, of which the use may be beneficial to the public, belongs, therefore, to the public, is quite a new doctrine," Webster said, referring to the ruling of the state court. "Whoever appointed a legislature to administer his charity? Or whoever heard, before, that a gift to a college, or hospital, or an asylum, was, in reality, nothing but a gift to the state?"

Confiscation is what Webster called the legislators' action. Besides, he pointed out, the words in the Constitution said, "No State shall pass any . . . law impairing the obligations of contracts."

"If the Constitution be not altogether waste paper it has restrained the power of the legislature in these particulars," he said.

He went on to argue that the state could not, under its own Constitution, judge a man without a trial and then deprive him of his property, as the State of New Hampshire had done to the trustees. A corporation, he insisted, had the same rights as an individual and its charter, being a contract, was its property.

"The case before the Court," Webster said, "is not of ordinary importance, nor of everyday occurrence. It affects not this college only, but every college, and all the literary institutions of the country . . . It will be a dangerous, a most dangerous experiment, to hold these institutions subject to the rise and fall of popular parties, and the fluctuations of political opinions."

At last Webster paused, his eyes filled with tears. When he spoke again his voice was choked. "Sirs, you may destroy this little institution. It is weak. It is in your hands . . ." he said. "It is, sirs, as I have said, a small college, and yet," he added, "there are those who love it."

Marshall leaned his tall frame forward to catch the words. Story peered sympathetically through his narrow spectacles. Bushrod Washington's pale, thin face looked paler still. The rest of the justices were obviously impressed. The Court, after hearing the other side, retired to consider the matter.

The overseers were agitated. They had underestimated Webster, they realized. The next day their agitation turned to consternation. Marshall announced from the bench that the Court had reached no agreement on the Dartmouth case and would have to continue considering the matter.

Then the overseers acted. They took the stagecoach to Baltimore, where they hired William Pinkney, the best-known attorney they could find. Pinkney questioned the overseers on the case for a whole week. Then, with characteristic vanity, he sent them back to New Hampshire assured that he would obtain a rehearing of the matter.

The Supreme Court justices, meanwhile, left Washington to go on circuit duty and then on their summer vacations. The year slipped away.

The Court met next on February 2, 1819. The spectators rose as six of the robed justices took their seats on the platform. Justice Todd was ill and was not there. As soon as everyone was settled, Pinkney leaped forward, prepared to demand a rehearing of the Dartmouth case, but Marshall did not give him a chance. The Court, he announced, had reached its decision.

Webster's heart must have pounded in his chest as the Chief Justice, who had written the Court's opinion, proceeded to deliver it.

As always, Marshall divided the problem into questions. Was the Dartmouth charter a contract protected by the Constitution? If so, had the act of the New Hampshire legislature violated that contract?

At first he said, "It can require no argument to prove that the circumstances of this case constitute a contract. An application is made to the crown for a charter to incorporate a religious and literary institution. In the application, it is stated that large contributions have been made for the object, which will be conferred on the corporation, as soon as it shall be created. The charter is granted, and *on its faith* * the property is conveyed. Surely, in this transaction every ingredient of a complete and legitimate contract is to be found."

Secondly, he referred to the newly formed university as "a machine entirely subservient to the will of the government." Dartmouth, he said, had been founded as a private institution under the control of private literary men who had the right to choose their own successors.

This was part of the contract which New Hampshire inherited from the Crown, "the obligation of which cannot be impaired with-

---

* Emphasis supplied.

out violating the Constitution of the United States . . ." he said. "The judgment of the State Court must therefore be reversed."

As would happen so often in the years ahead, a concurring opinion was delivered by Justice Story. The act of the legislature, he declared, was unconstitutional and therefore void. Partly because of Story, Webster had won. Dartmouth had won. And it is clear now, after a century and a half, that the country had won also.

The boys at Dartmouth went wild with excitement and fired off a cannon ball that tore through the trees, roaring the news of Dartmouth's victory to the surrounding countryside. Mr. Hopkins, a noted lawyer of the day, said, "Dartmouth was founded by Eleazar Wheelock in 1769 and refounded by Daniel Webster in 1819."

With the decision on this case the integrity of contracts was proclaimed throughout the land. The states were reminded that they must abide by their obligations and keep their contracts. The resultant atmosphere of security for investors and industrial dreamers provided the assurance necessary for the growth and development of the nation.

Today, when a corporation gets a charter, state laws and court decisions set limits as to what the agreement includes. In granting a charter, legislatures specify as part of the agreement the conditions under which the state may revoke it. But the great principle still stands that the contract, as written, must be kept.

Here, too, as in the Bank case decided a month later, John Marshall used the power of the Court to set aside an unconstitutional act of a state. Without this power, the Government as we know it could hardly have survived. Instead, the United States might quietly have disintegrated.

Bibliography
Principal Sources, Case 3

BOOKS

Beveridge, Albert J., *The Life of John Marshall.* Boston & New York. 1916.

Farrar, Timothy, *Reports of the Case of the Trustees of Dartmouth College against William H. Woodward.* Portsmouth, New Hampshire. 1819.

Lord, John King, *A History of Dartmouth College.* Concord, New Hampshire. 1819.

Thompson, Seymour D., *The Dartmouth College Case. A Study.* New York. 1898.

Warren, Charles, *The Supreme Court in United States History.* Boston, Massachusetts. 1935.

UNITED STATES FEDERAL RECORDS

Trustees of Dartmouth College v. Woodward, 4 Wheaton, 518.

☆ CASE 4 ☆

Gibbons v. Ogden

The Court Confirms Federal Jurisdiction over Interstate Commerce

---

"Here are three states almost on the eve of War."

ATTORNEY GENERAL WILLIAM WIRT, 1824

THE TIMES
AND THE ISSUES

No weapon that Congress holds to protect the nation's economy is greater than its power to regulate interstate commerce. Through this authority the Federal government determines the rules by which people from every corner of this vast nation conduct their business dealings. The framers of the Constitution foresaw and provided that only the Government of all could properly be entrusted with safeguarding the interests of all the people in their interstate transactions. But it took the Supreme Court to make sure that Congress' essential powers in this field could not be wrecked by the greedy wishes of local groups.

The first great case involving individual rights and interstate commerce was heard in 1824. It was docketed as *Gibbons v. Ogden,* and it grew out of a series of lively battles between the owners of the first steamboats. Here follows the tale of the forays.

☆

"An Asylum for Thieves and Robbers"

Colonel Aaron Ogden's sail-propelled ferry took off from his own dock at Elizabethtown, New Jersey. For years the sailboat had safely carried the townsfolk across the swift currents of New York Bay. Then, on a gloomy morning in 1808, Ogden stood helplessly by while his former customers climbed aboard John Livingston's new steamboat, the *Raritan*. Ogden choked with indignation.

He could see that the *Raritan*'s huge wooden wheels were scooping up more than the white spray of the bay. They scooped up, as well, huge profits for the Livingstons. Out of these profits John Livingston intended to give the Colonel a small allowance for the use of his dock, but Colonel Ogden was much too spirited to be summarily retired in this manner. He was only fifty-two, and although a bit heavy, his body was still as healthy as his complexion.

Ogden would have liked to be providing competition with a steamboat of his own, but the Livingstons and Robert Fulton had managed to get a law passed in New York that no one could navigate the state's water using any ship propelled by steam or fire without a license from them. Ogden considered the New York law an affront not only to himself but to all sailors, and particularly to all citizens of New Jersey. He planned to do something about it.

Whatever he did, he felt that he could count on support from the townsfolk. He came from an old Elizabethtown family and had taught in the town school. During the revolution, Aaron Ogden had led Elizabethtown men into battle all the way from the Brandywine to victory at Yorktown. Since then, he'd become an attorney and served his neighbors for part of one term in the United States Senate.

Ex-Senator Ogden studied both the design of the steamboat and the history of the Livingston-Fulton monopoly. As early as 1798, John's brother, Robert Livingston, had asked the New York legislature for the exclusive right to run steamboats in New York. The lawmakers had called his plan to build a boat propelled by steam "an idle and whimsical project," but they had listened to him because Livingston was a celebrity. He had been New York's first chancellor, and an important judge, and had administered the oath of office to George Washington at that President's first inauguration.

Livingston had told the legislature that he couldn't afford to risk his capital in developing a craft of this nature unless he could count on later collecting all the profits from having the only steamboats in New York. He admitted that a John Fitch had once had a similar grant and had patented a steamboat that ran on the Delaware River. But Fitch, Livingston said, had either died or gone away without developing the craft into a usable commercial vessel.

The New York legislature granted Livingston his exclusive navigation rights provided that he could produce a usable boat propelled by steam in one year's time. He couldn't, and in 1799 the grant lapsed.

Then, in 1801, Robert Livingston went to France as President Jefferson's diplomatic minister. While arranging for the purchase of Louisiana from Napoleon, he met Robert Fulton, a slim, oversensitive, dreamy-eyed American of Irish extraction, with bushy hair. The inventor was working on a steamboat then, and needed money. Handsome, aristocratic Mr. Livingston had money, as well as the vision to see the possibilities of ships propelled by steam.

After meeting Fulton, Livingston insisted that the New York legislature renew the old law, this time granting him and Fulton the exclusive right to run steamboats in New York.

More years of toil followed, but on a clear August afternoon in 1807, Robert Fulton's *Clermont* took off from her moorings in New York's Hudson River. Skeptical spectators who lined the dock were not surprised when she went a short distance and then stalled, but an hour later, at two o'clock, Fulton got her started again. Gray smoke rose from her stack, her hissing engine forced her wheels through the water, and soon she was averaging five miles an hour —passing sailboats and luring curious people to the riverbank to stare and wave as she labored her way upstate. In thirty-two hours the *Clermont* reached Albany, her flags flying and mobs of thrilled men, women and children cheering her arrival.

A chastened and impressed New York legislature made good its earlier promise. In 1808, New York added other provisions to the original law. Any steamboat daring to enter New York without permission from Livingston and Fulton could be seized, and Livingston and Fulton could keep their monopoly going for thirty years. For some reason it did not occur to the legislature that by granting such a monopoly they might be interfering with the right of Congress to regulate interstate commerce.

A thirty-year monopoly! Up and down the coast, from New Jersey to Connecticut, boatmen were furious. Why didn't Livingston and Fulton have to rely on a patent like other inventors?

A patent would have given them exclusive, nationwide rights to their boats, but only for fourteen years. More important, a patent would have left other shipbuilders free to develop their own steam craft, provided that their vessels were sufficiently different from Fulton's. After all, Fulton's boat had followed Fitch's, and many other inventors had "steamboat fever." By what right did the Fulton-Livingston monopoly forbid *their* using fire or steam to move their ships! Seamen in New York complained. Seamen in Connecticut and New Jersey petitioned their legislatures to take vigorous action against the unfair monopoly. The cheers for Fulton soon turned to curses. Shocked sister states planned retaliatory measures against New York. The fight was on.

Ogden, searching for a way to break out of his own financial prison, was conscious that other seamen were in the same position. However, he had the ear of the New Jersey legislature. He was active in Elizabethtown politics and the Elizabethtown citizens were a lively force. They were so progressive that they were already laying sidewalks, and until the legislature had stopped them they had let both women and Negroes vote at an election. With the support of these forward-looking neighbors, Ogden was selected by the legislature to be the state's governor for one year starting in 1812.

Months before his term started, the New Jersey legislature provided Ogden with a weapon against the monopoly. It passed a law giving any citizen of New Jersey whose boat was seized under the Fulton-Livingston grant the right to seize any New York boat lying in New Jersey waters. Here was an open invitation to violence against the citizens of the sister state. Possibly Ogden had not suggested this legalizing of piracy, but being furious at the monopoly, he did rely on its effectiveness.

He conferred with a watchmaker in Mendham, New Jersey, named Daniel Dodd, who was fascinated with the idea of tinkering with large machinery and agreed to undertake the designing of a steamboat for him. Dodd moved to Elizabethtown and set up a work shop. There he took Fulton's plans and added an innovation of his own. He used four wheels instead of one on each side, and connected his wheels to each other by a shaft, so that one steam engine could propel all four.

The new steamship was to be called the *Sea Horse,* and a builder was still working on her large hull in the spring of 1811 when New York announced its answer to the New Jersey law: Any steamship violating the Fulton-Livingston monopoly was to be seized on the day it entered New York and be kept within the jurisdiction of the New York courts until after the subsequent lawsuit was settled. That meant that a captain lost his boat before he had a fair trial, and he lost it in New York where he couldn't retaliate.

For a long time, Ogden and Dodd ran the *Sea Horse* only in New Jersey waters, between Elizabethtown and Jersey City. Meanwhile, they anxiously awaited the outcome of a very important lawsuit. A Mr. Van Ingen was challenging the legality of the monopoly in the New York courts.

When Van Ingen lost, Ogden persuaded the New Jersey legislature to grant himself and Dodd the exclusive right to run steamboats in New Jersey waters—so he could license others. Actually, he took no money from those requesting New Jersey steamboat licenses. He used his grant only to strengthen his political position for his next move against New York. Then, at the proper time, Ogden asked the New York government for a hearing on the desirability of steamboat monopolies.

At six o'clock on the evening of February 26, 1814, members of a specially formed committee of the New York Assembly (lower House) gathered in their dim, candle-lit hall in Albany to hear New Jersey's ex-governor.

Ogden put forth all the showmanship he could muster. He explained that his motives in coming were purely patriotic. He had with him a tin engine model made by Dodd, but before explaining its purpose he held up a picture of "Poor John Fitch's" early steamboat. It had no wheels, but six paddles on each side like a canoe. Nevertheless, they were attached to a shaft moved by a steam-propelled disk in the boat. "It frequently worked [even] in rough weather," Ogden explained. Ogden then pointed to his engine model showing Mr. Dodd's shaft-connected wheels, which he assured the legislature was a great improvement on Fulton's design.

Dodd had as much right, he said, to build a boat better than the *Clermont* as Fulton had to improve on Fitch's invention.

Fulton's attorneys, Cadwallader Colden and Thomas Emmet, seethed as Aaron Ogden, now an aging soldier statesman, developed his arguments and held the committee members in fixed attention. He had been preparing this presentation for months and they had had—they wrote later—only six hours' notice of the meeting. Satisfied that there was much in Fulton's work that was not original, the committee recommended to the full assembly that the monopoly be discontinued. The assembly then referred the proposition to the New York senate.

The senators acknowledged that the great but eccentric John Fitch had run a steamboat. Many of them remembered that he had called himself Lord High Admiral of the Delaware. But Fitch's boat had not been a commercial success. On the contrary, it appeared that country folk had been repelled when the weird contraption had come up the river with neither sail nor oarsman. The senators felt that the state's honor was at stake in keeping its promise to Livingston; and so, in spite of everything Ogden had said, the monopoly remained. The war between the states remained. To make matters worse, the monopoly's lawyers now went before the New Jersey legislature to fight Ogden.

On a snowy day in Trenton, Thomas Emmet, a once poor religious refugee from Ireland who had become an eminent attorney, spoke for Fulton. He called for the repeal of Ogden's licensing privileges, shouting, "Repeal this law or you will make your state an asylum for thieves and robbers." Ex-Governor Ogden, he insisted, was trying to rob Fulton of the fruits of his labors.

Ogden's young attorney answered that it was the duty of New Jersey to resist the operation of this oppressive system, which would convert its citizens into slaves of the state of New York.

Nevertheless, Ogden was beaten. New Jersey continued to legislate against New York, but not in Ogden's favor. His political party—the Peace party of 1812—was out of power. Thus the legislature of 1815 had no obligation toward Ogden and they repealed his grant.

Now his position was hopeless. His long struggle for all seamen's rights, his expensive boat and his attorney's fees had brought him close to bankruptcy. To cut his losses he paid the monopoly for a ten-year grant to run the only steamship from Elizabethtown to

New York. Thus Ogden gave up his fight and became himself a monopolist. He did not foresee that a fresh adventurer would soon challenge his newly purchased monopoly rights. Thomas Gibbons was the next ship owner to fight the monopoly system, and it was against Aaron Ogden that he warred.

☆

"*The Waters Are Free*"

When the Supreme Court justices examined their docket for the year 1824 they saw on the calendar an unusual case involving a steamboat. The suit was being brought by one Thomas Gibbons against ex-Governor Aaron Ogden of New Jersey.

As always, the justices were interested in the facts, so they read the history of the New York monopoly, starting with the grant to Fitch. They learned that in 1818, Thomas Gibbons, a politician and renowned duelist from Georgia, had decided to establish a steamboat line in competition with ex-Governor Ogden. Gibbons had fixed up a dock at the mouth of a creek within the limits of Elizabethtown and run his ship from there to New York. Incensed at this violation of his monopoly the ex-governor had gone to court and obtained an injunction against Gibbons, compelling him to stop his operation.

Gibbons had coped with the injunction issued against him in a most ingenious manner. Running his ship along the New Jersey coast, he had then deposited his customers at Ogden's Elizabethtown dock, where they could catch Ogden's boat to New York. Ogden did not object to that, since it increased his own trade, but John Livingston did. The Livingstons had sold the ex-governor the right to take passengers from Elizabethtown to New York, but not to serve passengers from all over New Jersey.

Livingston had taken both men to court, charging that they were partners combining to break the monopoly. The same agent in New York was selling rides for both their ships, and they were sharing the same dock. When both Ogden and Gibbons denied that they were partners, Livingston pointed out that in the course of making his stops, Gibbons was entering New York waters without permission from the monopoly. And once more Gibbons was enjoined.

Still resourceful and determined, Gibbons had now attacked the legality of the whole monopoly system. He fought especially the earlier injunction that had been issued against him at Ogden's request, which stopped him from running his boat from New Jersey to New York.

In the fall of 1819 he had met his adversary, Ogden, in court, and there the two adventurers and their attorneys had aired their dispute before New York's famous Chancellor Kent.

A small man with a large head, Kent, as he sat listening, appeared to be all brains; and indeed he was one of the most respected judges of his day. The Supreme Court justices were known to consult him on difficult cases. For years to come, his writings would be the handbook of law students hoping to pass the bar examination.

Ogden should have admired his opponent's courage. Ogden himself had steered clear of the courts during his own battle against the monopoly. Kent's views were well known. He believed in stopping society from stepping on the rights of individuals. He considered the Fulton-Livingston thirty-year grant as sacred private property to be respected.

Gibbons, however, produced a fresh and stunning argument. His boats, he explained, were enrolled at Perth Amboy in the United States coastwise trade. Therefore, he said, he was licensed to engage in interstate commerce, and under the United States Constitution interstate commerce could not be regulated except by Congress.

Kent considered the matter. He agreed that the Constitution gave Congress the power to regulate commerce with foreign nations and among the states. But, he said, a state could still give a grant of exclusive rights within its own borders. Therefore, he said, he could not see that the monopoly violated the Constitution. No state regulation, he said, stopped trading ships from coming into New York harbor. They simply could not be propelled by steam or fire in the state's waters without permission from Fulton and Livingston.

Of course, if at some future date the Livingston-Fulton grant interfered with an act of Congress, then the state law would have to yield to the power of the Federal government. That, the Chancellor thought, had not happened as yet—for a coasting license, he said, was not a license to engage in trade; it merely established the ship's nationality for tax and duty purposes. If the national lawmakers, he claimed, had intended the coasting license to be anything more than that, they would have said so. Therefore, Kent announced, he was ruling against Mr. Gibbons. The injunction against the Gibbons steamboats remained. Furious, Thomas Gibbons urged the Supreme Court to review the Chancellor's decree.

At the time, the justices had not yet ruled on the extent of Congress' powers under the interstate commerce clause in the Constitution. They decided to hear the case, and Gibbons persuaded the fashionable and brilliant William Pinkney to take his case; but Pinkney was destined never to make the argument, for shortly thereafter he died. Gibbons must have been overwrought, for he rewrote his will, leaving a legacy of $40,000 to have his case continued even if something should happen to him.

Ogden and Associate Justice Story had their own troubles in connection with the case. En route from Baltimore to Washington their stagecoach collided with a wagon and turned over, crashing into the roadside mud. Fortunately, nobody was seriously hurt. When at last on February 4, 1824, the attendants waiting at the side of the courtroom helped the justices into their robes (as yet they had no chambers to enrobe in), the Court assembled without one of the justices, Smith Thompson, who had properly decided not to sit, because of his family connections with the Livingstons.

Daniel Webster and Attorney General Wirt, who had agreed to speak for Gibbons, had good reason to be worried. The Court's respect for Chancellor Kent was well known to both of them. Besides, Thomas Emmet was appearing for the monopoly, and as Wirt wrote his brother, "Emmet's whole soul is in this case and he will stretch all his powers."

The one thing Webster hoped he would not hear Marshall say was, "It is admitted." He had told Story earlier, "When Judge Marshall says, 'It is admitted, sir,' I am preparing for a bomb to burst over my head and demolish all my arguments."

In spite of the case's handicaps, Webster started off brilliantly. He first paid a compliment to Kent's knowledge and competence. Then he described the belligerent atmosphere that existed between the states:

"By the laws of New York, no one can navigate the bay of New York, the North River, the Sound, the lakes, or any of the waters of the state, by steam vessel, without a license from the grantees of New York [the monopolists], under penalty of forfeiture of the vessel.

"By the laws of the neighboring state of Connecticut, no one can enter her waters with a steam vessel having such a license. By the laws of New Jersey . . . any citizen of that state . . . restrained under the New York law . . . shall be entitled to an action for damages, in New Jersey. . . ."

His concluding words were, in effect, "If there is no power in the general government, to control this extreme belligerent legislation of the states, the powers of the Government are essentially deficient, in a most important and interesting particular . . . if they [these laws] should be declared to be valid and operative, I hope somebody will point out where the state's right stops."

Webster's description must have reminded Marshall and the others of the mess that had existed before the Constitution was adopted. Then, states had passed customs duties against each other's products and used different systems of weights and measures, not only wrecking the country's commerce but also fostering such misery and rebellion as to almost terminate the nation's existence. Webster, of course, reminded the justices that the Constitution was written at least partly to halt the commercial warring between the states.

He next tackled Kent's argument that the monopoly did not interfere with any existing law or prohibition by Congress. Where Congress had not acted, he claimed, it had decided to leave the merchants free. Deciding not to make a rule is also part of regulating interstate commerce, he declared, and consequently, the absence of Federal regulation could not justify the states' making their own rules for the benefit of a few of the citizens of their own state. Kent's position, Webster said, implied dual control of interstate commerce, by both the states and the Federal government. "The doctrine," he said, ". . . is insidious and dangerous."

Furthermore, Webster explained, in this instance Gibbons had enrolled his ships in the coastwise trade. If that was all the license Congress required him to have, that was all the license he needed. He was authorized by the Federal government to engage in interstate commerce. And with this the state law interfered.

When Webster had finished, William Wirt arose and spoke clearly and precisely.

He said, "Here are three states almost on the eve of war; it is the high province of this court, to interpose its benign and mediatorial influence. . . . Sirs, if you do not interpose your friendly hand, and extirpate the seeds of anarchy which New York has sown, you will have civil war."

He might have added that by now Ohio had also passed laws excluding ships licensed under the New York grant from her waters, and at the same time the monopoly had taken steps to spread its tentacles over the Mississippi River, involving more states. Instead, he asked how this situation had come about. Why had Fulton and Livingston not relied on a legal patent? Because, Wirt concluded, the state had offered them better terms—terms that violated the rights of others and overstepped the bounds of state sovereignty.

Emmet then had his chance to reply. Naturally, he reiterated much of what Kent had said. He too was conscious of Kent's reputation. Then he amplified on Kent's position. "There is no grant in the Constitution giving the navigable waters peculiarly to the Federal government and not to the states within which they be," he declared.

He likened the granting of a steamship monopoly to the building and policing of roads, or the digging and managing of canals, or the regulating of stage coach travel, all of which the state had the legal right to handle. Emmet then made his most original argument. "The power given to Congress to regulate commerce with foreign nations, and between the several states, relates to commerce [only] in the proper acceptation of the term," he said. He added that what he deemed to be the meaning of the word commerce was "the exchange of one thing for another," or trade.

The power of Congress over commerce, Emmet claimed, could only be extended to cases of trading, and not to the mere transportation of passengers. Gibbons, he pointed out, was only navigating his ship for passengers and was not, he insisted, engaged in commerce or the exchange of goods.

Bowing, he took his seat, and the arguments were over.

From that moment on, newspapers all over the country speculated as to when the decision would be handed down and what it would be. Everybody in America seemed to care. The whole history of the growth of transportation was at stake and everybody seemed to know it. The New York *Commercial Advertiser* assured its readers that "inquiries are hourly made respecting the anxiously awaited decision."

More personal misfortune dogged the case. Marshall, returning from a visit with President Monroe, slipped and fell while stepping from his carriage, painfully dislocating his shoulder. He was at home trying to recover while an eager world awaited his final pronouncement on the steamboat case.

It was not until March 2 that he returned to Court, was warmly greeted and again took his seat. By then the justices had already agreed on their position in the steamboat controversy. Marshall, although still badly bruised and shaken, asserted his usual position of leadership and officially explained the Court's decision.

He pointed out first that Emmet had argued that carrying passengers was not commerce. Therefore, Marshall said, "it becomes necessary to settle the meaning of the word."

"The Counsel for the appellee [Emmet] would limit it to . . . buying and selling, or the interchange of commodities . . ." But, Marshall said, "it is something more: it is intercourse. It describes the commercial intercourse between nations, and parts of nations, in all its branches, and is regulated by prescribing rules for carrying on that intercourse. The mind can scarcely conceive a system for regulating commerce between nations, which shall exclude all laws concerning navigation. . . ."

Marshall reminded his listeners that the power over commerce, including navigation, was one of the primary objects for which the people of America adopted their government. He quoted the Constitution: "The ninth section of the first article declares, '. . . nor shall vessels bound to, or from, one state, be obligated to enter, clear, or pay duties in another.'

"These words have direct reference to navigation," Marshall said. And he insisted that they proved that the American people intended the word commerce to include all navigation as surely as if both words had appeared in the Constitution. That settled Emmet's argument that carrying passengers was not commerce.

Only two questions still remained to be settled. Could the states make their own rules for interstate traffic whenever Congress did not choose to act? And, if not, couldn't New York still impose the monopoly as part of running her own internal affairs? Emmet had said she could. Kent had thought so, too.

As Webster expected, Marshall made glowing remarks reminding his listeners that Kent was an eminent jurist.

Before he finished his presentation his voice began to weaken, enfeebled by the strain put on his health by his accident. The anxious spectators crowded closer to the bench to hear him quote the Constitution. Congress could control commerce, Marshall quoted, "with foreign nations, and among the several States, and with the Indian tribes."

Then Marshall explained, "It is not intended to say that these words comprehend that commerce which is completely internal, . . . But in regulating commerce . . . the Power of Congress does not stop at the jurisdictional lines of the several states. It would be a very useless power if it could not pass those lines. . . . If a . . . voyage may commence or terminate at a port within a state, then the power of Congress may be exercised within a state." Therefore Congress could, if it wished, regulate the steamboat traffic.

Marshall next evaluated Kent's argument that the states could still pass regulations on interstate traffic where Congress had not seen fit to act. Marshall repeated Webster's argument that Congress by not acting in a given situation was thus deciding that it wanted no action taken. Marshall said Webster's argument on this point had not been refuted by his opponents.

Marshall pointed out that besides, in this instance, Congress had passed an act—an act to enroll or license all ships or vessels to be employed in the coastwise trade. Since steamboats were not separately mentioned or excluded, Marshall said, "This act demonstrates the opinion of Congress, that steamboats may be enrolled and licensed, in common with vessels using sails. They are, of course, entitled to the same privileges, and can no more be restrained from navigating waters, and entering ports . . . than if they were wafted on their voyage by the winds, instead of being propelled by the agency of fire."

The New York law, then, by creating the monopoly, did indeed collide with the law passed by Congress. Marshall was sorry, very sorry, to override Kent, but the New York monopoly had to be voided.

Thus Ogden was beaten by his own original position. It could hardly have comforted him to know that he had been right in the first place in fighting the monopoly's control over interstate commerce. In fighting Gibbons he had spent more than he owned and it was all his neighbors could do to keep him from being jailed for debt. When he lost his steamship line they found him a job as customs collector. His friend Engineer Dodd went on developing steamboat engines and was killed when a boiler on one of his boats burst.

Gibbons later got into more scrapes. Uninvited, he entered a man's house to lure him into a duel, and as a result was successfully sued for trespassing. He had family troubles besides. But in the steamboat case he—and, fortunately, America—had triumphed.

The effects of Marshall's decision were immediately felt. A New Jersey newspaper rejoiced that "The waters are now free." Other northern papers described the steamboat passengers as "Exulting in the United States Supreme Court decision against the monopoly" —as well they might. Fares dropped, and within a year the number of steamboats running from New York to Baltimore multiplied from four to forty-three. Freed from the restrictions of monopoly, every major river in the country soon had its own steamboats, while New York harbor prospered as never before as more and more of these vessels plowed into her port.

In less than half a decade, the first locomotives were racing over railroad tracks. How could they have developed if the traveler and his goods could have been halted by the abuses of monopoly and crippling state regulation? After that, any state edict, tax law, license law, or special rule which could be shown to interfere with interstate traffic and the free flow of goods was promptly outlawed by the highest tribunal. Local groups could no longer benefit at the expense of the nation.

Today, whether a carrier in interstate commerce jets above the clouds, rolls over the highways or over the rails, or winds along underground in the form of an oil or gas pipeline, the power of Congress is there to protect the public from excessive rates or sharp business practices in interstate commerce. The telephone and the telegraph are similarly regulated, to promote the flow of travel, trade, and communication that helps unite the nation.

With his broad definition of the word commerce—including all business intercourse—Marshall not only freed the waters but infinitely strengthened the country and enhanced the people's welfare.

Bibliography
Principal Sources, Case 4

BOOKS

Colden, Cadwallader, D., *A Vindication.* New York. 1819.

Colden, Cadwallader, D., *The Life of Robert Fulton.* New York. 1817.

Davidson, Marshall B., *Life in America.* Boston. 1951.

Dickinson, H. W., *Robert Fulton, Engineer & Artist, His Life and Works.* New York. 1813.

Dictionary of American Biography. Published under the auspices of the American Council of Learned Societies. New York. 1943–58.

Fulton, Robert, *A Letter from Fulton to Aaron Ogden.* New York. 1814.

Hatfield, Edwin Francis, *History of Elizabeth, New Jersey.* New York. 1868.

Kent, James, *Kent's Commentaries on the American Law.* Boston. 1884.

Preble, George Henry, *A Chronological History of the Origin and Development of Steam Navigation.* Philadelphia. 1885.

Stockton, L. H., *A History of the Steam Boat Case.* Trenton. 1815.

Warren, Charles, *The Supreme Court in United States History.* Boston. 1935.

UNITED STATES FEDERAL RECORDS

Gibbons v. Ogden, 9 Wheaton 1 (1824).

NEW YORK RECORDS

4 Johns. Ch. 150 (1819).

NEWSPAPERS

New York Commercial Advertiser, March 12, 1824.

Niles Register, July 1818, Baltimore.

Savannah Republican, May 2, 1826.

☆ CASE 5 ☆

Ex Parte Milligan

The Court Declares the Rights of Civilians in Time of War

"The Constitution of the United States is a law for rulers and people, equally in war and in peace."

ASSOCIATE JUSTICE DAVID DAVIS, 1866

THE TIMES
AND THE ISSUES

As far as the Federal judiciary was concerned, the Civil War brought with it a fight within a fight. As Union troops prepared to battle Southern soldiers, the military and the Federal justices clashed over the rights of civilians in time of rebellion. The President as Commander-in-Chief, the nation's newspapers and the Congress all became involved when Chief Justice Taney declared that no army officer could hold a nonmilitary citizen prisoner without being subject to the courts and their power to invoke the rules of justice.

All over the land, men debated Taney's position, but because of the war's fury the issue was not subjected to a final ruling until after the guns were silenced. Then the question of the legality of the imprisonment of a Mr. Milligan came before the Supreme Court. The Milligan case represents more than the case of one suspected saboteur. It involves the rights of all Americans, and the episodes and arrests that preceded it are important to the tale. The story is part of the fight for justice in times of mass hysteria. It starts in Maryland six weeks after the outbreak of war.

"*The Body of John Merryman*"

In the wee hours of the morning of May 25, 1861, a Union captain and two subordinates acting under the orders of General William H. Keim picked their way through the darkness in Cockeysville, Maryland, north of Baltimore, where they located and forcibly entered the home of John Merryman. The home owner was well liked locally—an established citizen, active in many civic associations—but the soldiers were not impressed.

Cockeysville was full of Southern sympathizers, endangering Baltimore, which had to be held if the United States government was to survive. The city was an all-important link in the railroad line between New York, Philadelphia and Washington.

The three soldiers hauled Merryman out of bed and dragged him off, like a common criminal, to Fort McHenry. Inside the fort they turned their captive over to Major General George Cadwalader. Here, they said, was one of the leaders of a rebel drill corps.

Cadwalader was not comfortable with the situation and said so. A day later he wrote to Washington asking for instructions and explaining, "I directed the officers who brought the prisoner here to have more specific charges and specifications against the accused with the names of witnesses. I regret to say that I have not as yet been furnished with this information."

The General had good reason for not liking the position in which he found himself. Almost at once, Merryman's lawyer, George H. Williams, appeared, demanding to see the warrant under which his client had been arrested. Cadwalader could do nothing for his comrades in arms but refuse to show any papers.

The attorney thoughtfully weighed his next move. It was useless to run to a local Federal judge. A Union major had already defied Judge William F. Giles when Giles ordered the major to produce a runaway juvenile enlisted in the Union ranks. An official with more authority and prestige must be found. Williams rode to Washington and went to see the Chief Justice of the United States, Roger B. Taney.

Taney by now was an old man of eighty-four. His long frame was thin and bent, racked by his long fight against ill health and by the burdens of many years in office. Since he had been appointed by Andrew Jackson to succeed Marshall eight Presidents had come and gone. And months back, Taney's trembling old hands had held the Bible for President Abraham Lincoln to take the oath of office.

The Chief Justice listened, shocked, while Merryman's lawyer described the low ebb of justice in Baltimore, and then, in Merryman's name, asked for a writ of habeas corpus, one of the most sacred weapons in liberty's arsenal, which prevents a person's being illegally held or imprisoned. The Latin words *habeas corpus* mean "you may have the body," and a judge's writ of habeas corpus commands a jailer or custodian to bring the prisoner before the court. If the prisoner can then show that he has been illegally detained, he can win a release. Judge Giles had issued such a writ in order to interview the runaway juvenile and his writ had been ignored.

The outraged Chief Justice could have told Williams—if any law student needed to be told—that the cruel refusal of his Majesty's judges to issue writs of habeas corpus to the colonists had been one of the grievances that led to the American Revolution. As British subjects the colonists considered it their birthright to obtain "the great writ" whenever they were illegally arrested. It was out of fear that a strong Federal government would annihilate freedom that Patrick Henry had fought the ratification of the Constitution. And several states had demanded, as a condition of ratification, the later inclusion in the Constitution of ten amendments called the Bill of Rights. The Founding Fathers who demanded the adoption of the Bill of Rights seemed to have cases like Merryman's in mind, for in addition to freedom of religion, freedom of speech and of the press and the right to assemble or to petition the government for the redress of grievances, the Bill of Rights also guarantees every citizen the security of his person and house against unreasonable search and seizure. Every person accused of a crime, as Merryman was, is entitled to a fair and speedy trial and may not be deprived of liberty or property without due process of law—in other words, without a court action during which the government must obey all the rules passed to protect the rights of the accused.

In addition to all this, the original text of the Constitution provided that "The privilege of the writ of habeas corpus shall not be suspended, unless when in cases of rebellion or invasion the public safety may require it."

There was only one trouble. It occurrred to Taney that if he issued a writ answerable in Washington, then General Cadwalader might refuse to obey. The General might reply that a military officer could not leave his appointed district.

Taney was intent on not letting that happen. He departed at once for Baltimore. The Maryland city was familiar to the old Chief Justice. At stated intervals he sat there as a circuit judge along with Giles. The courtroom they used was in the old Masonic Building on St. Paul Street. From there Taney issued his writ. On Sunday night, May 26th, the court clerk delivered it. Cadwalader read that he was ordered to appear before Taney at eleven o'clock the next day and have with him "the body of John Merryman."

General Cadwalader made up his mind that he was not going to court. Instead, on Monday he sent an Army colonel, who appeared before Taney in full dress uniform, his sword dangling at his side. With stiff formality the colonel announced that the accused was charged by the military with holding a commission in a treasonous association of armed men and with avowing hostility to the Government.

The colonel also reported Cadwalader as claiming that "he is duly authorized by the President of the United States in such cases, to suspend the writ of habeas corpus, for the public safety. This is a high and delicate trust, and it has been enjoined upon him that it should be executed with judgment and discretion, but he is nevertheless also instructed that in times of civil strife, error, if any, should be on the side of safety to the country."

No speech could have been more horrifying to any judge. Soldiers, with their battlefield orientation, and their contempt for civilians in time of war, and their lack of judicial training, could not be allowed to imprison private citizens or jeopardize the lives and freedom of possibly innocent people merely because they were erring on the side of safety.

When Taney indignantly asked for John Merryman, the Colonel said he had no instructions except to deliver the message he had just recited. Then he turned and marched from the courtroom. The bewildered and infuriated Chief Justice immediately ordered the court clerk to issue an attachment of contempt of court against

General Cadwalader "returnable before me at twelve tomorrow." This time Taney did not send the court clerk. He sent the United States Marshal to deliver the order.

Word of the proceedings spread from mouth to mouth across Baltimore. Even Marylanders who were loyal to the Northern cause declared Merryman's treatment "shocking" . . . "disgraceful" . . . "unheard of." Whether he was guilty or not was beside the point. Nothing could be proved without a fair trial.

Long before the doors of court opened on Tuesday an excited crowd gathered on St. Paul Street. As soon as the doors were opened, the people pushed their way in. When Taney took his seat on the bench at noon the room was packed.

General Cadwalader did not appear. Taney called on the marshal for an explanation. Apologetically, Marshal Bonifant stepped forward. He had gone to the fort gate and sent his card in to Cadwalader with a sentry. "The messenger," he said, "returned with the reply that there was no answer to my card. I . . . could not serve the writ as I was commanded. I was not permitted to enter the gate."

Taney bristled. To the spectators he said, "A military officer has no right to arrest and detain a person not subject to the rules and articles of war." If he does, he is subject to the Court's authority, Taney claimed.

If Cadwalader had been anything other than a general, Taney said, the marshal could have formed a posse to go after him. But since Cadwalader commanded an army, this was not practical. Taney announced that he would write his opinion of the case and not only file it with the clerk but also send a copy to the President of the United States, calling upon him to perform his Constitutional duty to enforce the laws—in other words, to enforce the process of the court.

Taney then dismissed the assembly and trudged to his son-in-law's town house a few blocks away to write his opinion. For the President's benefit, the Chief Justice stated the case as he saw it: "a military officer . . . issued an order to arrest a citizen of Maryland upon vague and indefinite charges, without any proof, so far as it appears." But this was not all. An officer, in defying a writ of habeas corpus issued by the Court, had claimed that his actions were authorized by the President. "I certainly listened to it in some surprise," Taney wrote, "for I had supposed it to be one of those points of constitutional law upon which there was no difference of opinion and that it was admitted on all hands that the privilege of the writ could not be suspended, except by Act of Congress."

If the officer was not exceeding his authority, then, Taney declared, "the President has exercised a power which he does not possess under the Constitution." Taney went on to point out that President Jefferson had not claimed the power to suspend the writ even when Aaron Burr formed an army to overthrow the government. In fact, not even the monarch of England was allowed to suspend the writ of habeas corpus. This was a power "which could not have been lawfully exercised by the sovereign even in the reign of Charles the First," Taney said.

He quoted statements by former Chief Justice Marshall and Associate Justice Story as to the inviolable nature of "the Great Writ." He quoted paragraphs from the Bill of Rights guaranteeing the safety of all citizens from unreasonable search and seizure, and from imprisonment without a legal trial. These rights, he pointed out, not even Congress could suspend—much less the military. Besides, the courts in Maryland were not closed by the war and there was, therefore, no excuse whatsoever for the Army to be interfering with justice.

If the power which the Constitution had confided to the judiciary could thus be usurped by the military on any pretext, Taney said, "The people of the United States are no longer living under a government of laws but every citizen holds life, liberty and property at the will and pleasure of the Army officer in whose military district he may happen to be found." Hence, Taney said in reporting his own actions, "my duty was too plain to be mistaken." He ended as he had promised, by charging the President to fulfill his oath of office and take care that the laws be faithfully executed, including respect and enforcement for the Court's process.

When he had finished, the Chief Justice rose to take his paper to Court, telling his grandson that he might be in prison at Fort McHenry at nightfall but he was going to Court to do his duty.

Taney was not arrested. His words merely evoked screams of treason, printed in the nation's papers. Many editors scribbled hysterically. Chief Justice Taney was using court procedure to shield Southern sympathizers. Their cries drowned the voices of the more sober editors who felt that Taney had acted to uphold the law.

The *Baltimore American* made the boldest statement in behalf of

Taney. "A government which is fighting to maintain the Constitution," it said, "should interpose no arbitrary action to suspend or interfere with the rights plainly guaranteed under it." How, in other words, could young men be called to the colors to fight for the right if the highest officer in the land was wiping out the most fundamental tenets of the Constitution?

President Lincoln did not make his answer directly to Taney. Instead, he defended himself in a message to Congress. The President referred to the desperate situation brought on by Southern sympathizers, and asked, "are all the laws but one to go unexecuted, and the Government itself to go to pieces, lest the one [law] be violated?" President Lincoln said he would consider his official oath of office broken if he should allow the Government to be overthrown when disregarding a single law would have tended to preserve it. Furthermore, the President argued, he was not convinced that only Congress could suspend the writ. The Founding Fathers could not have intended that every danger should run unchecked when Congress was not in session.

What the President did not add was that he was in no mood to be lectured on human rights by Roger B. Taney. It was Taney, Lincoln bitterly remembered, who with his Southern plantation upbringing, had announced the hated Dred Scott decision from the Supreme Court bench. According to that decision a slave was not a citizen and so not entitled to bring an action in court. And the hard-won Missouri Compromise, forbidding slavery north of the 36/30 line, was unconstitutional. It deprived slave owners of their property. So Taney had said in 1857.

It did not impress the President that Taney, being a literal man, had taken the position that the Constitution recognized slavery, and so, if the practice was to be abolished, it would have to be done by Constitutional amendment and not by the Court's pretending to legislate from the bench. To Lincoln the owning of human flesh was indefensible and the Court's ruling had further spread the blight across the country. He showed his disregard for Taney by now asking Congress to uphold the executive's actions.

That left it up to the lawmakers to approve the President's action or depict him as a treacherous usurper of power before the war-torn nation. Furiously, senators and congressmen debated the question among themselves. Emotions boiled over, and the decision was repeatedly postponed.

Finally, begrudgingly, after a month's delay, a rider was added to an Army pay bill approving the President's past proclamations and thus legalizing his suspension of the writ. After that, Congress passed its own law. The President was given wartime power to suspend the privilege of habeas corpus, but with provisos. A person suspected of endangering the public safety could be kept in a military prison, but only until the civilian grand jury met in the local courthouse in that area. Meanwhile, the Army officers in charge of prisoners were to supply the civilian court with a list of all nonmilitary persons being held and give all the particulars concerning their arrests. If the grand jury failed to indict a suspect, the prisoner could ask the local judge for an order that would force the military to bring the man before the court for a hearing and discharge.

In other words, the privilege of the writ of habeas corpus, the rights of free men, and the cruel lessons of the past, including the spectacle of innocent people hauled off by soldiers to die, forgotten, in dungeons—all these things were too important for Congress to ignore, even in wartime. Some form of protection for the guiltless had to be continued. Unquestionably the congressmen and senators supposed that their legislation had settled the question. It didn't.

John Merryman was unusually fortunate. A year after he was captured, the Government decided that Baltimore was no longer a danger area, and the Army released him to the civilian authorities. Thus the question of the jurisdiction of the military over civilians was left undecided.

But as wartime sabotage and treachery increased, as Northern losses mounted, as the bloodletting and hatred intensified, there were more instances of improper arrest. In many areas martial law was declared and the military held tribunals for the prosecution of civilians whose rights were completely ignored. Not until the Union troops subdued the Confederate forces and the gunsmoke cleared did the constitutionality of these trials come up for a judicial ruling. Then, at long last, the Supreme Court found itself compelled to make a decision. It had to condone or condemn the incarceration of an alleged spy named Lambdin Milligan. At last Taney's issue involving military interference with civilian justice came up for review.

★

Freedom Was His Client

It was a far different Court that examined the facts in the Milligan spy case from any Taney had known throughout most of his tenure of office. The newspapers had called the Taney Court pro-Southern, and indeed many of the old justices did come from the South, but even before Taney died in 1864, fate handed President Abraham Lincoln the opportunity to appoint four associate justices to the High Court. Staunch Union men they were—men Lincoln could count on to have no sympathy with Southern rebels.

Justice David Davis was one. He had been a Lincoln supporter even before Mr. Lincoln won his nomination as a Presidential candidate. Davis, genial, smiling and sociable, and never happier than when he was rounding up a wagonload of constituents to take to a political rally, had been a strong support for the lean and sober Lincoln during campaign days. Davis was a real vote-getter. As an Illinois judge, he was much admired.

After Taney's passing, Davis and the other three recent appointees welcomed their next Chief Justice: Salmon Portland Chase was picked by Lincoln out of the President's own Cabinet. Chase was a fighter. Years back, his antislavery tirades had evoked from his fellow Republicans the cry of "Radical," but Chase unwaveringly persisted in his views. An ambitious attorney, he came to the bench somewhat sorrowfully, giving up all hope of ever occupying the White House.

For a time Congress had increased the Court's membership to ten justices, but again there were only nine.

This vigorous new Court met in a nearly new courtroom. With the enlargement of the Capitol in 1860, the justices were at last freed from their dingy basement quarters. They not only held Court in what had been the roomy Senate Chamber, but also at last had a robing room where they could dress for Court out of sight of the public. An upstairs office had been decorated for their use, and to it came the papers in the Milligan affair.

Milligan, according to General Alvin Hovey, was party to a treasonable conspiracy planned by the so-called Sons of Liberty. The Sons, the justices agreed, were a truly heinous group. Evidence had been piling up against them for a long time. When the steamer *Taylor,* loaded with supplies for the Army, burst into flames at her Louisville, Kentucky, dock; when enrolling officers calling men up for the draft were found shot; when vital military information was leaked to the Confederate enemy; and when an increasing number of citizens were successfully fed propaganda calling for a negotiated peace with the South, Judge Advocate General of the Army Joseph Holt had been able to attribute all the mischief to that dangerous group.

In July, 1864, a remorseful character who confessed to having once belonged to the Sons, wrote to the *Eaton* (Ohio) *Gazette* that the members aimed to rule the government or destroy it. "If they are drafted," he divulged, "they will use their guns against the Federal soldiers." Certainly the group was a menace. The question before the justices was whether it had been properly established that Milligan had participated in any of the crimes of these desperadoes.

According to Army reports, matters relevant to the Sons had come to a climax near Milligan's home in Indiana. On a peaceful June day a party of well-dressed civilians marched themselves up to the gates of the Union Army camp outside of Indianapolis and told the soldiers on duty that they had to see the Brigadier General. The matter was urgent.

They waited, visibly anxious—possibly feeling conspicuous among the many uniformed men who milled about. After some little time they were admitted to the sparsely furnished quarters of Brigadier General Henry Carrington.

They were terrified. They freely admitted it. The Sons of Liberty were ready to strike, they said. The General questioned them calmly. There was much he needed to know. Who were they? How did they know about the Sons? What did they know?

Several of them spoke in turn. They were registered Democrats. As such, they had been solicited by recruiting agents for the Sons, and pressured to join the subversives. This much of the story was logical. A well-briefed agent for the Sons of Liberty could roll off his tongue all the reasons why a Democratic party man of those days ought to be dissatisfied with President Lincoln's Republican administration. Mixed in with his sales pitch was always a hefty dose of Southern propaganda, states' rights, and anti-abolition. The general by now was familiar with the organization's tactics. An agent, once having revealed who he was, would swear a prospective member to secrecy and obedience, making it quite clear that the secret order was not averse to resorting to bloody violence to silence anybody in whom the officers had misplaced their confidence.

As a rule, the leaders of the Sons kept subordinates totally ignorant of the organization's intentions. How much information, then, could his visitors have, the General wondered?

The Democrats said they had plenty. The Sons were going to seize the Government arsenal on the night of August sixteenth. They were going to rescue the Army's prisoners of war, arm the prisoners and lead them to a prearranged junction with rebel forces from outside the state. With this combined might the Sons expected to capture Indiana and make it capitulate to the Confederacy. Everything was ready. Each key man had been instructed by his superior as to his assignment—whom he should murder—what else he should do. Either the General asked for the names of leaders or the Democrats volunteered them. In any case, Milligan's name was mentioned during the discussion of the anticipated violence.

Thus warned, the Army prepared to head off the outbreak. The General assigned his men to watch the incoming trains and roads. Every possible precaution was taken, and the rebel reinforcements never arrived. The uprising never took place. August ended and Indiana was not in Confederate hands and not a battle area.

In October the state was in the throes of a political campaign leading up to the November presidential election. General Alvin Hovey had been placed in command of the military district. According to Hovey, the city of Indianapolis was filled with enemy officers and corrupt officials bribed by rebel gold. They gathered, he said, late at night to plot their treason.

Hovey himself had been described by General William Tecumseh Sherman as an overambitious man. This may explain the action he took. He may have expected to exploit the excitement always engendered by a political campaign to make a name for himself, but his own explanation of his behavior was, "Knowing the danger and necessity of the hour, I smote as many of the heads of the hydra as my sword could safely reach."

General Hovey ordered his men to invade the home of Lambdin Milligan. The soldiers seized Milligan and dragged him back to

Army camp. There they shoved him into a prison cell. It was the Merryman affair all over again, except that this time, as commanded by Hovey, the soldiers tried Milligan themselves before a military commission that met on October 21.

Milligan insisted that he was a civilian not in any way connected with the Army, and that they could not try him. Hovey paid no attention. Hovey's officers dutifully found Milligan guilty of treason. Their orders were that he and several of his alleged associates be hanged on the parade ground.

Milligan's lawyer, Joseph McDonald, raced to Washington. He would never forget the events of that stay in the nation's capital. Later he related the experiences to William Herndon, who included the story in a biography of Abraham Lincoln.

As McDonald told it, early one evening he managed to get in to see the President. Since there were other callers waiting to speak to the Chief Executive, McDonald expected the interview to be short and feared that he could accomplish little. Still, he intended to do his best for Milligan.

As it happened, McDonald, like Lincoln, had for many years argued cases before the circuit courts in the prairie districts and the President remembered him. The two men compared memories and exchanged anecdotes of their old circuit days, talking and joking in the comfortable White House reception room until nearly eleven o'clock. At last, McDonald smoothly introduced the subject of his client and tactfully pressed Milligan's case.

The Chief Executive did not, however, override Hovey's authority in ordering the military trial. He upheld it. But it was Lincoln's idea—so McDonald said—that if the war ended before Milligan's execution took place, it would then be safe to commute the sentence to a prison term. All McDonald won from the President was a little time. Time, though, was a fateful ally in Milligan's cause.

The local grand jury met in the Indianapolis Courthouse on January 2, 1865. They transacted the business before them and twenty-five days later adjourned. They had not considered Milligan's case because they had not received a list of civilian prisoners from the Army.

The circuit court met in May. Milligan was to be hanged on May 19. On May 10, McDonald made one more bold attempt to save Milligan. He went before the circuit judges and asked for a writ of habeas corpus. The two judges who made up the circuit bench

listened to his request, discussed it, and as time ticked away, argued
with each other as to what ought to be done. More time was con-
sumed and the circuit judges still failed to agree on what their
proper course should be. Finally they sent the question up to the
Supreme Court for a ruling.

The Army officers who had considered the case closed now
found, to their astonishment, that a final ruling on the question was
again pending. By this time the war was over and everybody was a
lot calmer. The officers resigned themselves to obeying the circuit
court's order, which was to delay Milligan's execution until word
came from the highest tribunal. Time again worked wonders for
Milligan. In June, President Andrew Johnson commuted Milligan's
sentence from the death penalty to life imprisonment. He was moved
under guard to the Federal penitentiary in Ohio.

Meanwhile, his attorney prepared to fight for his freedom before
the Supreme Court. The case was called on March 6, 1866, and
argued until March 13. McDonald did not try to handle it alone. He
called in two other lawyers to bulwark his position. One attorney
was a brilliant young man arguing his first Supreme Court case. He
was a future President, James A. Garfield. The other attorney was a
tall, distinguished, elderly gentleman, with matted dark hair. He
was Jeremiah Black.

Pacing up and down in the narrow clearing that edged the high
dais on which the nine justices sat, Black poured out his arguments.
He needed no brief and he looked at no notes. As his ringing voice
filled the chamber his words seemed to spring spontaneously from
his soul. Milligan might be a heinous character, but Black felt that
freedom was his client. If constitutional liberty was to survive, Milligan could not be deemed guilty without being given a fair trial.

Black called out the names of tyrants of old who had slaughtered
the innocent in the mere hope that the guilty were among them. He
traced man's long struggle to fashion laws that would be a protection from such ruthless persecution.

More quietly Black spoke of the wisdom of the Founding Fathers
of the Constitution who, he said, had provided against this very
villainy. The military were never meant to be independent of and
superior to the civilian authorities. They were obligated by law to
supply a list of their civilian prisoners to the grand jury. Instead, in
this case, they had usurped power to deprive Milligan of his right to
a fair trial. This could not be tolerated in freedom's name.

Black was quickly answered for the government by Attorney General James Speed and Benjamin F. Butler, who argued the necessity of wartime vigilance—who reminded the Court of the young men drafted for military service, subjected to the arbitrary will of their officers and shot on the battlefield without any trial.

Like Black, they, too, held the attention of the justices they faced. While arguing, Butler must have looked over the bench and tried to gauge what these colorful men in their black silk robes were thinking. Associate Justice Nathan Clifford was the most conspicuous—a man of gigantic girth. He was a pre-war Democratic appointee, as were Justices Samuel Nelson, Robert C. Grier and James Wayne. The others evaluating the validity of Lincoln's military courts were Lincoln appointees. They were Noah H. Swayne, Samuel F. Miller, Stephen Field, Davis and Chief Justice Chase. All listened in silence.

Milligan had to wait only three weeks for the justices to make up their minds. They were unanimous in their opinion: The military commission that had tried Milligan, they announced, was illegal. The full text of their opinion was withheld until later. Davis was going to write it and he wanted time to say exactly what he meant.

In mid-December Davis delivered his historic ruling from the bench. Strangely, it was the words of the now deceased Taney that weighed most heavily on the mind of Lincoln's old colleague and on the minds of his fellow justices. Davis said, as Taney had, "Martial rule can never exist where the courts are open . . . It is . . . confined to the locality of actual war." Military officers could govern only where all civil authority had been overthrown. They could rule by martial law only until the courts had been reinstated. If they attempted under any other circumstances to hold court for civilians it was a grave usurpation of power.

"One of the plainest constitutional provisions was, therefore, infringed when Milligan [a civilian] was tried by a court not ordained and established by Congress, and not composed of judges appointed during good behavior." In Davis' opinion, only civilian justices holding life appointments were free to judge objectively, free from the pressures of an aroused populace, free from the dictates of a commanding officer.

"Another guarantee of freedom," Davis said, "was broken when Milligan was denied a trial by jury. . . . a country preserved at the sacrifice of all the cardinal principles of liberty is not worth the cost of preservation."

All the justices were agreed that the President by proclamation could not authorize this military tribunal in a state like Indiana where no war existed. The President is bound by the law, they said. The majority went further and said that Congress under the Constitution could not legalize such military trials of American residents except where the war's devastation had closed the courts. "The Constitution of the United States," they said through Davis, "is a law for rulers and people, equally in war and in peace . . . and under all circumstances."

Then Davis noted the Government's argument that the exigencies of the war necessitated the suspension of individual constitutional liberty and the sacred Bill of Rights. Said Davis, "No doctrine, involving more pernicious consequences, was ever intended by the wit of man. . . . Such a doctrine leads directly to anarchy or despotism." He went on to tell the Government lawyers that the Founding Fathers had foreseen that troublesome times would arise when the people would be restive and constitutional liberty in peril. The Framers of the Constitution wisely provided against this very tragedy by means of laws—the laws of the Constitution and the Bill of Rights, he concluded.

Milligan, then, whether guilty or not, had to be released and set at liberty. There was no other way to guarantee that future decent men and women yet unborn could not be brutally, mercilessly abused by tyrants who could commit any atrocity and rely for vindication on a populace deranged by the devastations of a troubled hour.

A writ of habeas corpus was issued to the warden at the Ohio penitentiary. He obeyed it, and Milligan walked out a free man. More important, a bulwark of American Constitutional liberty had been firmly established.

Bibliography
Principal Sources, Case 5

BOOKS

Clayton, Mary B., *Reminiscences of Jeremiah Sullivan Black*. St. Louis. 1887.

Dictionary of American Biography, Published under the Auspices of the American Council of Learned Societies. New York. 1943–1958.

Hart, Albert Bushnell, *Salmon Portland Chase*. New York. 1899.

Herndon, William Henry, *Herndon's Lincoln; The True Story of A Great Life*. Chicago. 1889.

Richardson, James Daniel, compiler. *Messages and Papers of the Presidents*. Vol. 17. New York. 1917.

Steiner, Bernard Christian, *Life of Roger Brooke Taney*. Baltimore. 1922.

Swisher, Carl Brent, *Roger B. Taney*. New York. 1935.

Tyler, Samuel, *Memoir of Roger Brooke Taney*. Baltimore. 1872.

Walker, Charles Manning, *Life of General Alvin P. Hovey Together With A Sketch of Ira J. Chase*. Indiana. 1888.

UNITED STATES FEDERAL RECORDS

Ex Parte Merryman, Federal Cases Vol. 17, Federal Case 9, 487.

Ex Parte Milligan, 4 Wallace 2.

U.S. War Department, *Official Records of The Union and Confederate Armies in The War of the Rebellion, Series II*, Government Printing Office. 1880–1901.

PRINCIPAL NEWSPAPERS

Baltimore American, May 29, and June 4, 1861.

Baltimore Exchange, May 4, 1861.

Eaton (Ohio) *Gazette*, July 7, 1864.

National Intelligencer, May 29 and May 30, 1861.

MAGAZINES

Dent, Thomas, "David Davis of Illinois" *American Law Review*, Vol. LIII, 1919.

☆ CASE 6 ☆

Northern Securities v. United States

The Court Insures Citizens' Protection from Monopolists

"We draw the line against misconduct, not against wealth."

PRESIDENT THEODORE ROOSEVELT, 1902

THE TIMES
AND THE ISSUES

Railroads! All over the United States people were furious at the railroads. During the 1870's and 1880's railroads and monopolists were annihilating small businessmen. The typical railroad traffic manager, hectically trying to show his boss that he could please the richest customers, offered to hand money back to the big shippers when they paid their freight bills. Because of these rebates, the big shippers were able to lower the cost of their wares, monopolize the market and bankrupt their small competitors. Then the big shippers became the tyrants of the earth. With their competition out of the way they dictated their own terms to consumers and laborers alike.

Not all the monopolists were railroad-bred. Bigness was the trend of the era. At the same time, railroad practices and railroad favoritism did lead to a series of catastrophes. When railroads began merging into huge combinations capable of controlling the nation's whole economy by their grip over the nation's trade routes, President Theodore Roosevelt was impelled to act. The first mighty blow he struck against them was called the Northern Securities case.

☆

"The Public Be Damned"

When our story begins, late in the nineteenth century, suave, neatly dressed agents of the Standard Oil Company could be seen calling at the offices of one independent oil refinery after another. Seated across a conference table from a refinery owner in Cleveland, Philadelphia, Pittsburgh or New York, each gentleman courteously delivered a message from his boss, John D. Rockefeller: "Sell out! Or be crushed out."

Each Standard agent could assure his doomed host that gaunt, thin-lipped John D. was as able as he was willing to make good his threat. Everyone knew that Rockefeller was getting hefty rebates from the railroads. This enabled Mr. Rockefeller to slash the prices of Standard's oil and undersell all comers to the market place.

This he did. As relentlessly as a winter wind blows down the last of the autumn leaves, he forced one independent refiner after another to sell or shut down. When an abandoned building went up for sale, Standard was likely to have a purchasing agent on the spot. Often, all Rockefeller wanted was to dismantle the place.

By 1880 Standard had a monopoly. Rockefeller controlled ninety per cent of all the oil refineries in America. It made a man feel small, helpless and bitter. It made him wonder what had happened to the American dream—what had happened to the right of the small operator to be in business for himself and to be his own boss. In other industries, too, the dream was vanishing. Railroad rebates bred monopolies among the grain dealers, in the slaughtered-meat industry and—to everybody's great discomfort—in the coal industry.

The fall of 1883 found horrified New York housewives being warned by their local coal dealers to buy hastily. The cost of winter warmth was going up. After turning the pages of a weekly magazine called the *North American Review,* the housewives learned why. The previous July, railroad barons and monarchs of the coal industry had met for lunch in sunny Saratoga, a fashionable summer resort. Seated in comfortable, plush chairs in their luxurious parlor, the tycoons had conspired. They had agreed on how much coal they would permit to reach the market and at what price. If a reader's fury could have heated a house, many a New York family would have been cozy in its drafty brownstone abode that winter. And it wasn't only the cost of coal that upset the housewife. The wood in her ornately carved furniture; the meat, the fruit and the vegetables on her dinner table; the wool in her shawl and the cotton in her floor-length skirts—all were transported by rail. All these items could fall into the hands of railroad-created monopolists, and become prohibitively costly. It was enough to make anyone anxious. The railroad held a sledge hammer over the family's standard of living.

And the housewives were not alone in their anger. Angry farmers found that the lords of the railroads owned the tall, sparsely-windowed elevator buildings where the ripe wheat and corn were stored. When a grower hauled his crop by horse and wagon to the elevator, the railroad was charging so much for loading and storing the grain that it squeezed all the profit out of the farmer's toil. Besides, the traffic managers made up for the cut rates they offered customers shipping from big cities by demanding exorbitant prices to haul freight to and from small towns—where often there was only one railroad with no competition.

Thus the railroad barons ruined farmers and small businessmen, forcing workers to swarm to the big cities where they piled into the slums, and glutted the city labor markets, making it easier for the hated monopolists to depress wages further, spreading misery everywhere. Their attitude seemed to be summed up by the remark attributed to rail king William Henry Vanderbilt: "The public be damned."

The unhappy people begged their Government for help. According to his colleagues, United States Senator Shelby Cullom of the Interstate Commerce Committee received so many petitions against railroads he couldn't carry them down the corridor "without walking bowlegged." Local and state officials were equally deluged with mail. At last, impelled by public pressure, the engine of governmental investigation began to move. Hearings were called before committees in Washington and in the state capitols. Railroadmen were summoned to answer the question "How were rates set?" and to be further questioned on their part in the devastating rise of monopolies.

For an interminable period, the public thought the politicians seemed more willing to hold hearings, take testimony and talk than to act. Few people grasped what a mammoth task it was (as it still is) to put reins on a great industry. When the rural states tackled the problem by fixing railroad rates, the Supreme Court nullified the state laws. The states, the justices reminded everybody, were not privileged to interfere with interstate commerce. Congress alone held that power.

Congress then tried to grapple with the difficulty. Congress passed the Interstate Commerce Act of 1887 forbidding the railroads to agree to give rebates. Three years later Congress, also under its power to regulate interstate commerce, passed the Sherman Anti-Trust Act of 1890. This time the legislators were aiming directly at the monopolists. Persons, combinations of persons and trusts were forbidden to make contracts or form "conspiracies in restraint of trade." No one and no trust was to monopolize or attempt to monopolize the nation's commerce. The trusts were especially mentioned because they were huge corporations organized to gain control over smaller businesses by holding their stock.

It all proved useless. The industrial tycoons and railroad barons evaded the acts. They relied on help from the courts, where the justices were loath to deprive these empire builders of their rights to do what they pleased with their own property. The only real brake on the conduct of railroadmen was the competition they faced from each other.

Then a devastating incident occurred that rocked the nation, just at the time railroad millionaire James J. Hill was surging ahead with his own plans to make himself an invincible lord of the nation's trade routes—a supermonopolist.

Unlike most railroad men, Hill had received no public subsidy or government land grant. He had started his business career as a fatherless boy of fourteen clerking in a country store. Later, as a pudgy, high-foreheaded middle-aged man, he liked to recall how he had braved the Indians and the elements to lay his track across the wilderness, sustained by the hope that towns needing railroad service would follow his trail. He often reiterated how he had irrigated dry lands and imported good British cattle to help his customers. After all, it had cost him a lot to become a success. Hill was deeply offended at any suggestion that the Government or anyone else should interfere with him. As he saw it, since Government officials had not helped him build his railroad empire, it seemed unjust that they should control it.

Besides his own railroad, the Great Northern, which stretched from Puget Sound to the Great Lakes, Hill was the railroad expert for the Northern Pacific, owned by his financier friend, John Pierpont Morgan.

"Jupiter, King of the Gods" was what other tycoons called banker Morgan. When Morgan spoke, his words were orders, and the rich men of Wall Street obeyed—partly because they were afraid of Morgan, partly because they thought everything Morgan touched turned to gold. Hill, they believed, had reached the pinnacle of success by being associated with such a wizard, but Hill didn't think he had reached the pinnacle. He decided in 1900 that he needed to own the Chicago, Burlington & Quincy Railroad in order to run his trains into Chicago. To get it, he tackled another giant of the roads, Edward H. Harriman.

Mr. Harriman was a mild-looking, bespectacled gentleman, but with a business head as hard as his steel tracks. He ruled more than two-thirds of the railroads of the Northwest and had no intention of bucking any more competition from James Hill. Mr. Hill already controlled nearly a third of Northwestern rails, and when Hill started to buy into the Burlington, Harriman tried to bid him out of it. But the Burlington stockholders, who were proud of their railroad, were wary of Harriman. If Harriman ran Burlington, they thought, he might destroy it to fatten the business take of his Union Pacific. They joined forces with Hill.

As Hill could not afford all the Burlington stock he needed to control the road, he simply resold most of his purchase to his Great Northern and Morgan's Northern Pacific. Everything seemed to be neatly settled, but Harriman wasn't to be that easily beaten.

Late in the spring of 1901, Harriman hit back. He gathered together a group of his Wall Street broker friends, explaining that since Morgan was in Europe this was the perfect time to strike at Hill. Harriman sent the crowd down to the stock exchange to buy a controlling slice of Northern Pacific. By gaining control of Northern he expected to gain control of its new subsidiary, Burlington, automatically. It was a daring scheme typical of that tycoon.

As the brokers bid for the stock the price rose—and rose again. Wall Street manipulators saw the upward trend. Greedily, they sold to their customers more shares of Northern than they owned, expecting to buy it later after the price dropped back. By the time Hill realized what was happening, Harriman was nearly in control of Northern Pacific. Its price had risen from $85 a share in January to $160 in May.

Frantically, Hill wired Morgan in Germany. Then, with the banker's money and his own, he went into the market to buy back his railroad. The bidding went up to $1000 a share. Hill cursed but was willing to pay any price. His life's work was at stake.

Edward Harriman didn't care, either. He was gambling to bury two of the biggest men in the railroad game, and he was backed by John D. Rockefeller.

The manipulators, who had sold huge quantities of Northern that they didn't own, now had to buy the stock in order to make promised deliveries. To get the money, they sold everything else they held, no matter how low the price. As a result, the prices of all securities other than Northern came crashing down. People who had put their savings into those stocks suddenly saw their holdings drop in value. Panic reigned as family heads found that they were ruined. Even large fortunes were wiped out as the giants warred. And there was an even louder cry that the railroad "robber barons" must be curbed.

Then Morgan came forward with a new design to enhance even further the power of the railroad men. Hill and Harriman, he ordered, were to combine forces. He summoned his attorneys into his glass-walled office at the bank and they came running like pages waiting on royalty. What did Mr. Morgan want?

Morgan wanted them to form a trust. The company was to get ninety-seven per cent of Northern Pacific stock and seventy-five per cent of Great Northern stock. It would thus control both roads. Best of all, Morgan said, "It would be so wealthy nobody could ever buy it."

In return for giving up their railroad securities in these two lines the former owners were to receive stock in a new trust to be called the Northern Securities Company. Hill was made president and Harriman a director of Northern Securities.

Thus the giants were united. A common interest was to replace competition. Together they held the hugest, strongest railroad combination in the world. Men who already wielded more might than they could wisely handle were to be mightier than ever. To Hill, it was a big step toward his dream of being invincible. To

Harriman, it meant the enlargement of his empire. The greatly impressed attorneys flattered Morgan that his plan was truly unbeatable. There were handshakes and congratulations on all sides.

However, in the White House, Theodore Roosevelt, the hard-riding veteran of the Spanish American War, had been appraising big trusts and monopolies for a long time. He looked with foreboding at the Northern Securities Company, which he realized was a supermonopoly of all the railroads of the Northwest. It was also a possible steppingstone to complete control over all American railroads—and thence to a stranglehold on the nation's trade and economy. The President realized that if this happened, the fortunes of all the men and women in the nation would be in the power of reckless manipulators like Rockefeller, Harriman, Morgan and Hill. He decided that the unbeatable must be beaten.

☆

"That Was the Very Object of the Law"

Early in 1902 Hill and Morgan received a sudden and severe shock. The bad news came over the Wall Street ticker tape late in the afternoon of February 19, in the form of an announcement by United States Attorney General Philander Knox:

> Some time ago, the President requested an opinion as to the legality of this merger [of Northern Pacific and Great Northern] and I have recently given him one to the effect that, in my judgment, it violates the provisions of the Sherman Act of 1890.

The Attorney General went on to say that a court action against the Northern Securities Company and against Hill and Morgan was in preparation.

To the dazed tycoons the message meant that the President was out to enforce the almost forgotten antitrust law—and Northern Securities might not be the only monopolistic trust to be smashed by the judge's hammer. Morgan and Hill were not the only big dealers who were worried. All over Wall Street men talked of nothing else.

They were sure that Theodore Roosevelt's words to his Attorney

General were a lot stronger than the Knox statement would indicate. Knox, who had been a successful corporation lawyer given to dignified, cautious statements, took himself and his official position very seriously—too seriously for some.

Anyone familiar with the two personalities could easily conjure up a picture of Roosevelt thundering against those malefactors who combined and conspired to gain a dictatorship over the transportation of the nation's freight.

Knox had undoubtedly explained for the President's benefit the difficulties of winning a court case. Only seven years back the Supreme Court had emphatically refused to order the dissolution of a trust in the Knight sugar case despite the fact that the directors of the trust owned the stock of enough companies to control ninety-five per cent of the nation's sugar refining.

The sugar trustees, the justices had ruled, did not have to worry about the Sherman Anti-Trust Act. The piled sacks of sweet white crystals rode the freight cars from state to state only after the refining was done. The refiners, then, were not in interstate commerce, and the Sherman Act only applied to interstate commerce. Couldn't the justices now rule that the mere holding of stock by the Northern Securities crowd was not interstate commerce?

The justices had held that since many companies not owned by the trust were still grinding sugar, there was no monopoly. In the same spirit they could say that Hill and Morgan did not own all the railroads in America. Wall Street men liked to remember that only one justice had dissented in the Knight case—only one lone voice had been raised in protest from the bench. It was the voice of Associate Justice John Marshall Harlan. The ultraconservative position of the other eight justices had made a dead letter of the Sherman Act.

To many confident financiers it seemed that what Roosevelt now wanted Knox to do seemed almost superhuman. He wanted Knox to persuade the justices to broaden their viewpoint and reverse themselves. It was as gigantic a task as remaking the economic philosophy of an era. Most economists, like the justices, still believed in the *laissez-faire* theory of letting business do what it wished.

The energetic President refused to let that stop him. Roosevelt, therefore, with the help of his Attorney General, mapped out his campaign against this new form of economic tyranny.

Before the case could reach the Highest Court Knox would have to battle out the issues in a lower court. He planned to start his action in the Federal court in St. Paul, Minnesota. The President was to bolster the cause by delivering a series of speeches that would make the issue clear to the nation.

Meanwhile, Mr. Morgan, in his office at J. P. Morgan and Company, was calmly assuring brokers that Northern Securities was still a safe investment. He and Hill, he said, were fully prepared to win any legal fight. Having so spoken, Morgan took the next train to Washington to see if he could talk the President out of the "attack." Senator Chauncey Depew, himself a wealthy railroad man, arranged the interview between Morgan and the President in the parlor of the White House. Wall Street's "Jupiter" found that he had underestimated his opponent.

"If we have done anything wrong," he said to the President, "send your man [meaning Knox] to my man and they can fix it up."

"That can't be done," the President told him.

It was typical of a Wall Street tycoon to treat the President of the United States as he would a rival operator and act as if Roosevelt could be induced not to enforce the law. The Wall Street point of view had to be changed. The President was sure of that!

The case, however, ran into complications before it ever started. Governor Samuel Van Sant of Minnesota ordered his Attorney General, W. B. Douglas, to start an action against the Northern Securities Company similar to the one being planned by Knox and Roosevelt.

The state case came into the Federal court in January.

Minnesota had a law forbidding a railroad to buy control of a parallel or competing line and Northern Pacific and Great Northern were parallel lines. As Douglas explained to Judge William Lochren, Morgan and Hill were evading the law. They had handed the stock of both transportation systems over to one company, the Northern Securities Company, which was incorporated in New Jersey. The State Attorney General asked the Court, "Can a corporation organized under the laws of New Jersey use its corporate powers so as to violate or overthrow the constitutional enactments of a sister state?" To Minnesotans the very idea was impossible.

That wasn't all. The two lines thus merged, Douglas charged, constituted a monopoly under the Sherman Act. What was a monopoly if not a combination so strong that it could abolish competition? That, Douglas reported, was what was developing in Minnesota.

Farmers had complained to traffic managers of the Great Northern Railroad that the service was deteriorating. They threatened to take away their business and give it to the Northern Pacific. They were told, Douglas informed the court, that "It made no difference to the Great Northern whether it or Northern Pacific got the business."

Here was monopoly at its worst, with competition abolished. Douglas called witnesses to prove his point. Farmers Addison Leech, Ewald Weidman and Theodore Koch all took the stand. Since the merger, they said, sidings had been discontinued, leaving a man to get his crops to a loading station miles away as best he could. Freight trains no longer came on time. Farmers waited hours to get a car. Worst of all, the farmers were all convinced that the two lines would now conspire to raise rates.

Of course, Hill and Morgan gave their attorneys answers to all this. Hill insisted that the sidings weren't economical. Yes, there had been a scarcity of freight cars but that was being corrected. Morgan said he "never knew two lines that didn't compete." His main interest in forming Northern Securities was to stop raids like the Harriman affair. "We weren't going to have that fighting in Wall Street," he said.

The attorneys for Morgan and Hill convinced Judge Lochren, who ruled that Northern Securities was not a railroad buying a competing line but merely a stock-holding company. The judge's words were a terrible blow to the Federal government's cause.

Knox carried on the legal preparations for his own case, but now, he labored under the handicap of the Lochren court record.

Not all the testimony he wanted was taken in Minnesota. One spectacular act in the drama took place, not in St. Paul, but in Room 70 of the New York City Post Office Building. The room was so jammed with reporters and photographers waiting in a carnival mood for the famous Mr. J. P. Morgan to arrive for questioning before a special examiner that the United States marshal had to order the gentlemen of the press to put out their cigars.

Morgan arrived confident and chipper, even prompting the questioning attorney, George Lamb, as to what questions to ask. Then, in his expansive mood, he made a fatal admission. Northern Securities, he said, represented a "community of interests."

He did not seem to realize that this statement contradicted his claim that Northern Securities was merely a stock company and not a monopolistic merger in restraint of trade.

Attorney Lamb, with complete calm, picked up the cue. "What is the community of interest theory?" he asked.

Morgan boldly answered, "that a certain number of men owning property can do what they like with it."

"Even," Lamb pressed, "though they own competing lines?"

"Even though. . ." Morgan insisted.

Meanwhile, Congress passed a new law providing that monopoly cases involving matters of public importance had to be argued before at least three judges. The case was therefore moved from St. Paul to St. Louis where, on the appointed day, four judges heard Assistant United States Attorney James M. Beck insist that the difference between one railroad's buying a competing line to form a monopoly and Northern Securities' buying a controlling interest in two parallel lines was the difference between tweedledee and tweedledum.

Then the advocates for the United States voiced the President's fear. If what Northern Securities was doing was legal, Hill and Morgan could buy control of every railroad in the country. By controlling freight rates they could control the country's entire economy and become more powerful than the United States government.

At last, on April 9, 1903, Judge Amos Thayer spoke for his brethren. "The Securities Company," he agreed, "accomplishes the object which Congress has denounced as illegal. . . . It destroyed every motive for competition between . . . natural competitors." The stockholders of the Northern Securities Company, he pointed out, would never permit competition between the two railroads. It wasn't to their interest to have rates go down or services increase merely to let one of their own lines take customers away from another line they also owned. He enjoined the directors of Northern Securities from carrying on their business. How the Supreme Court justices would rule was now anybody's guess.

Chief Justice Fuller, who had rendered the decision in the Knight case, was still on the Court. His full head of hair and bushy moustache had turned white, but he was still a sturdy gentleman. Harlan, who had dissented, was also still there. He was a massive man in size, in intellect, and in spirit. The other justices loved and respected him. Associate Justice David Brewer, with a humorous twinkle in his eye, told a Washington dinner party, "Harlan retires to rest at night with one hand on the Constitution and the other on the Bible." Nevertheless, Brewer along with the others had rejected Harlan's views in the Knight case.

Three new faces in the Court were Joseph McKenna, a conservative Republican from California; Rufus W. Peckham, a railroad attorney from New York; and the great judge from Massachusetts, Oliver Wendell Holmes, who had startled conservatives by saying, "I think the strike a lawful instrument in the universal struggle for life." As Roosevelt had hoped, Holmes continued to voice liberal views from the bench, but the President had made a wrong prediction on only one issue: Holmes was not against big railroad combinations. He felt that they were inevitable. Holmes could not find that the Hill-Morgan merger kept anybody else out of the railroad business.

Consequently, although Roosevelt was not at first aware of it, with the appointment of Holmes in 1902 he was stacking the odds against himself in the Northern Securities case.

In August of that year the President took to the road, traveling through the New England states and the Middle West, telling the story of the big fight to all who would listen.

With boundless energy, the President moved from one community to another under the relentless summer sun, and mounted the speaker's platform to tackle the difficult job of alerting the citizenry to lawless monopoly without letting his campaign turn into a rabble-rousing exercise against all successful businessmen. His was not a war against wealth and industry but a war against lawless industrial combinations built to knock down competition and monopolize trade.

Again and again, in as many ways as he could devise, the President repeated what he had said earlier to Congress: "The captains of industry who have driven the railway systems across the continent, who have built up our commerce, who have developed our manufactures, have on the whole done great good to our people. Without them the material development of which we are so justly proud could never have taken place. . . .

"We draw the line against misconduct, not against wealth. . . .

"I believe the monopolies, unjust discriminations which prevent or cripple competition . . . and other evils in trust organizations . . . which injuriously affect interstate trade can be prevented under the power of Congress to regulate commerce . . ."

The crowds got the message.

Only eight months after the ruling in St. Louis, the momentous case went into its final battle before the Supreme Court. The justices, no longer required to go on circuit duty since a reform bill passed in 1891, were able to docket it promptly for December 14.

It was a clear day, not too cold, and after the justices had dressed for the occasion in their official robing room, the police held back a considerable crowd behind thick ropes while the gentlemen of the bench, in all their dignity, filed down the Capitol corridor to their courtroom. Fuller led the procession, followed by Brewer, Harlan, Holmes and all the others, including the latest Roosevelt appointee, William R. Day, of Ohio. The venerable age of most of them added to the solemnity of their appearance, although the dashing Justice Holmes was youthful-looking at sixty-two.

The attorneys seemed to sense that the decision would be a close one as their voices rose in anxious argument. Both sides knew the peril of their position. From this court there was no further appeal. Whatever was decided here would be final, and from this day forth, monopolies would either be controlled or flourish unchecked. Everything that could be said must be said. The arguments used in the lower courts were repeated; the lower court judges were quoted; the lawyers reviewed the Knight case and the history of railroads.

The Government called for enforcement of the Sherman Act to protect the little man. It declared that New Jersey must not be permitted to grant a charter allowing the recipient to monopolize interstate commerce.

The Hill-Morgan's attorneys insisted that they were not running a conspiracy in restraint of trade or competition. They had a charter, which gave them the same rights as an individual under law. How could an individual conspire with himself? An individual, moreover, could do what he wanted with his own property. The

Hill and Morgan men could not see how Congress could stop that.

They were so emphatic on this point that when Knox's turn came, he said he did not deny "the very spirited contention that the construction the Government puts upon the law in question interferes with the power of people to do what they will with their property. . . . That was the very object of the law."

The question was, did too-powerful monopolies destroy the rights of others? Then, as the other Government lawyers had, Knox cited the dangers of such a situation, but at last his voice, too, died away and the justices retired to consider the problem in solitude.

Later, they discussed the case together in the Court conference room on the floor below as four young page boys sat on the couch and listened to the making of history. Not until years later, when a decision leaked before it was due to be announced, were the youths barred from the secret deliberations of the elderly justices.

This time it was a heated discussion that the boys heard, for the justices violently disagreed. Four, led by Harlan, were entirely on the side of the Government. Four, led by Holmes, were entirely against Knox's position. Brewer was writing his own opinion. As it turned out, though his words were milder than those of Harlan, Brewer did side with Roosevelt and Knox.

Finally, on March 13, Harlan read the majority decision. With devastating clarity he told Jupiter's men, "If Congress has not, by the words used in this act, described this and like cases, it would, we apprehend, be impossible to find words that would describe them." The Government had won its case. The justices had grasped the danger.

Harlan reiterated the words of Roosevelt's Attorney General. "The government charges that if the combine was held not to be in violation of the act of Congress, then the efforts of the National Government to preserve to the people the benefits of free competition . . . will be wholly unavailing . . . placing the public at the absolute mercy of holding corporations."

The law, he said, could not be thwarted by merely getting a New Jersey charter of incorporation. "No State," he added, "can, by merely creating a corporation, or in any other mode, project its authority into other States, and across the continent, so as to prevent Congress from exerting the power it possesses under the Constitution over interstate and international commerce. . . ."

Thus was the St. Louis Circuit Court's ruling upheld. Northern

Securities Company had to be dissolved. It was a great day for competitive free enterprise.

Of course, not all the monopolies immediately fell like birds shot out of the sky. But March 13 marked the end of their heyday. Later, the meat trust and the tobacco monopoly were broken up by the courts, and in 1911 the Standard Oil Company was forced to give up many of its affiliates.

Farm organizations and labor unions are stronger today than they were then, and Government regulation of interstate commerce is stricter. There is no longer any question of whether the Sherman Act can be enforced. It is enforced. Congress has passed additional antitrust acts, and the Federal Trade Commission and the Antitrust Division of the Department of Justice are responsible for their enforcement.

The housewife goes to the store confident that no one manufacturer can eliminate all the others and then jack up prices. The laborer in most industries has the assurance that there will always be a choice of many employers. The small merchant can vend his wares without being destroyed by favoritism in transportation charges.

Most important is the fact that no group is so strong, economically or otherwise, that it cannot be made to obey the law. The Government, designed for the people, has not fallen by default into the hands of a few huge combines. America has met the challenge to representative government brought about by industrial evolution.

Bibliography
Principal Sources, Case 6

BOOKS

Beard, Charles A. and Mary R., *The Rise of American Civilization.* New York. 1946.

Biddle, Francis, *Mr. Justice Holmes.* New York. 1943.

Butt, Archie, *Taft and Roosevelt.* New York. 1930.

Butterfield, Roger, *The American Past.* New York. 1947.

Lloyd, Henry D., *Lords of Industry.* New York. 1910.

Meyer, Balthasar Henry, *A History of the Northern Securities Case.* University of Wisconsin Bulletin, Economic and Political Science Series. 1906.

Pringle, F. Henry, *Theodore Roosevelt.* New York. 1958.

Pyle, Joseph Gilpin, *The Life of James Hill.* New York. 1917.

Roosevelt, Theodore, *The Works of Theodore Roosevelt.* New York. 1926.

United States Library of Congress Reference Service, *The Constitution of the United States of America, Analysis and Intepretation,* U.S. Government Publication. Washington, D.C. 1953.

UNITED STATES FEDERAL RECORDS

United States v. E. C. Knight Co., 156 U.S. 1 (1895).

Congressional Record, January, 1901; and January, 1902.

Documents and Court Records of the Northern Securities Case. U.S. Department of Archives. Washington, D.C.

United States v. Northern Securities Co. 120 Federal Reporter, 720, April 9, 1903.

Northern Securities Co. v. United States 193 U.S. 197, 1904.

U.S. Congress, *Senate Report 46,* 49th Congress, 1885–1886.

NEWSPAPERS

New York Times, February 20 and 21, 1902.

MAGAZINES

Baker, Ray Stannard, "The Railroads on Trial." *McClure's Magazine* (Dec., 1905; Jan. and March, 1906).

Pollock, Frederick, "The Merger Case and Restraint of Trade." *Harvard Law Review* (Jan., 1904).

Whitney, Edward B., "The Northern Securities Company." *Yale Law Journal* (June, 1902).

☆ CASE 7 ☆

West Coast Hotel Co. v. Parrish

The Court Upholds Laws for the Benefit of Wage Earners

"Liberty implies the absence of arbitrary restraint, not immunity from reasonable regulations . . ."

CHARLES EVANS HUGHES, 1937

THE TIMES
AND THE ISSUES

"A law embodies beliefs that have triumphed in the battle of ideas," said Associate Justice Oliver Wendell Holmes. In America, even before the Constitution was written, one of these triumphant ideas was that man was at liberty to do what he wanted with his own property. For a long time employers interpreted this to mean also that they were entitled to be free from any interference in determining the hours, working conditions and pay of their hired workers. As long as enterprises were small and the printer's apprentice and the blacksmith's boy expected to run their own shops someday, this interpretation was generally accepted.

Then came the giant industries, with their expensive machines requiring a fortune to finance, and a large segment of the population faced the prospect of being hired help for their entire lives. If the people in the new laboring class were not to live like slaves they had to demand rights that they had never had before. This meant contesting some of the long-estabished prerogatives of the private property owner.

Changing the economic attitudes of the nation was slow going. It took courageous men who could accept change. Among these men were two great Supreme Court justices who, contrary to the beliefs of their associates, maintained that laws could be passed to regulate a man's own business so that his employees would also have their liberties—and this without depriving Americans of their cherished right to acquire and enjoy private property.

Here is the story of those two justices, Oliver Wendell Holmes and Louis Dembitz Brandeis, and of their long campaign for the constitutionality of labor legislation—a campaign that won out at last in a series of cases heralded by *West Coast Hotel Co. v. Parrish*.

"Made for People of Fundamentally Differing Views"

The dining room was a sea of motionless gentlemen in black tuxedos. Forks lay untouched on empty and nearly empty plates. The glasses had ceased their bell-like tinkle. Associate Justice Oliver Wendell Holmes was speaking.

The listening gentlemen gathered here in New York were, like Holmes, Harvard University Law School alumni, and this was their annual dinner. The year was 1913. The words that riveted their attention referred to the Supreme Court justices.

"We, too, need to learn to transcend our own convictions," Holmes said, "and leave room for much that we hold dear to be done away with . . . by the orderly change of law."

His words were the key to Holmes' repeated conflicts with his colleagues on the bench. Holmes believed that the people's elected representatives were entitled to pass whatever new legislation "the crowd" wanted, provided that the new laws were within the Constitution. Whether he or other judges liked the legislation was beside the point.

Holmes believed this so deeply that he was willing to fight for it. He was, in a quiet way, fighting at this dinner, trying to put his convictions across to this fashionable assembly of successful men. Many of them must have swallowed hard at the thought of "much that we hold dear to be done away with." They took a good look at their recalcitrant speaker—tall, with a head of white hair and a white moustache that gave him a well-deserved distinguished air. Life had readied him for his battle of ideas.

As a boy in Boston Holmes had needed tact and patience to get along in the home of his strict and famous father, the author of *The Autocrat of the Breakfast Table* and the great poem "Old Ironsides." As a young man and an army officer in the Civil War he had developed not only his courage but also the will to persist. He was wounded at Ball's Bluff and again at Antietam, and after long, trying days in the hospital had gone back into the thick of it, to be wounded once more at Fredericksburg.

When he was mustered out Holmes had studied law. On a glorious Memorial Day in windswept New Hampshire in 1884 he once addressed a post of his fellow veterans of the Grand Army of the Republic and told them why.

"What other calling," he said, "gives such scope, to plunge so deeply into the stream of life, to share its passions, its battles, its despair, its triumph both as witness and as actor . . .

"In law as in a magic mirror we see reflected not only our own lives but the lives of all men who have been."

He had picked a law career because it summoned him to combat in life's most significant battles, and Holmes had not been on the Supreme Court bench three years when on a bleak spring morning he heard the warriors' bugle in the case of the New York bakers. In his imagination he visualized the bent backs of the men as they strained to push heavy troughs loaded with soggy white dough across a hot and steaming kitchen. Theirs was an exhausting job.

The New York Legislature had been persuaded to pass a law prohibiting bakery employers from working their men more than ten hours a day. When one baker upstate in Utica, Joseph Lochner, had violated the statute for the second time, a New York judge levied a fine of $50 against him and the bakery owner took his case to the Supreme Court.

Lochner's attorney protested that the New York legislation was grossly inequitable; it favored the workers. Holmes, as was his custom, took out a notebook and a pencil. He bent over and began to write as the attorney continued.

The Fourteenth Amendment, passed after the Civil War, forbade the states to deny any person the equal protection of the law, the lawyer reminded the Court. It also extended the Fifth Amendment to bind the states by forbidding them to deprive any person of life, liberty or property without the process of law—and due "process" meant according to the rules set up for the protection of individual rights. As Lochner saw it, a biased legislature deprived him of his liberty to make his own contracts with his men, thus depriving him of control over his own property.

Old Justice Rufus Peckham, speaking for the majority of the Court, agreed: ". . . there is no reasonable ground for interfering with the liberty of persons or the right of free contract, by determining the hours of labor, in the occupation of a baker." He considered the act merely meddlesome. Bakers were able to assert their own rights and care for themselves without the protecting arm of the state.

Holmes disagreed, but he understood Peckham's thinking. Peckham, like the other justices, had been educated in Herbert Spencer's descriptions of *laissez-faire* philosophy—Spencer warned governments to leave business alone. Society would function best, he said, if every man was left on his own to struggle to do his utmost in making and marketing his wares or selling his services. If the government helped those who were at a disadvantage in the fight for prosperity, then the assisted citizens would lose their own initiative and self-reliance, make feebler efforts in their own behalf and become dependent. Besides, Peckham's teachers reasoned, the founders of this country wanted a government that was limited in power and would leave private property unmolested. The only excuse for state laws was to protect the public health, safety, or morality. They were not to interfere with a man's liberty to sell his skills, run his mill or manage his employees. A man's business was his private domain by natural right.

New York's social legislation was contrary to everything Peckham had been brought up to believe. Holmes, knowing this, tried to hit at the heart of Peckham's reasoning as he delivered one of his famous dissents.

"Some of these laws," he said, "embody convictions or prejudices which judges are likely to share. Some may not. But a constitution is not intended to embody a particular economic theory. . . . It is made for people of fundamentally differing views, and the accident of our finding certain opinions . . . shocking ought not to conclude our judgment upon the question whether statutes embodying them conflict with the Constitution of the United States."

Holmes thought that liberty, or the right of every citizen to do as he pleased, as referred to in Peckham's opinion, stopped where everybody else's rights began. He said,"I think that the word liberty in the Fourteenth Amendment is perverted when it is held to prevent the natural outcome of a dominant opinion, unless . . . the statute proposed would infringe fundamental principles . . . of our people and our law."

The New York law, Holmes thought, should have been upheld as

the will of the majority. It was not in any way contrary to the
Constitution as he saw it. Lochner, he felt, was not being deprived
of his property rights. He still owned his bakery.

Holmes knew as he spoke that he would not sway his associates.
Their minds were made up. The old soldier was maneuvering for a
victory in the far, far future. With infinite patience he was speaking
to posterity and calling on men not yet grown to right the wrongs of
this day. The words he chose were weapons to be thrust at injustice
by the social warriors of a generation still to come.

Twice more in the next ten years Holmes raised his voice in
dissent to champion the will of the wage-earning majority, and both
times he was calling to the future. The cases were very much alike.

One of them was docketed as *Coppage v. Kansas.* It involved a
Kansas law which made it a misdemeanor for any employer to
coerce, require, or demand that a man agree to stay out of a union.

This time Justice Mahlon Pitney, a middle-aged Republican from
New Jersey, read the opinion of the Court. The Kansas law was
unconstitutional. It interfered with freedom of contract. Earlier,
Pitney had pointed out that in the case of *Adair v. United States* the
Courts had thrown out a similar statute passed by Congress.
Holmes had dissented then; now he dissented again.

He felt that even the contents of contracts were subject to regulation by the lawful representatives of the people. In addition, he
said, "a workman not unnaturally may believe that only by belong-
ing to a union can he secure a contract that shall be fair to him. If
that belief, whether right or wrong, may be held by a reasonable
man, it seems to me that it may be enforced by law in order to
establish the equality of position between the parties in which liberty of contract begins . . ."

Trying to guide the future with forceful dissents was often exasperating work, but during the trying years between the Lochner
and the Coppage cases one especially exciting day brightened the
life of Oliver Wendell Holmes. It was the fifteenth of January,
1908.

Before the Court appeared a tall, wiry and energetic attorney
with hair that would not lie down on his head and eyes that sparkled
with the vision of a new future. Holmes was happily acquainted
with this advocate. He was Louis Dembitz Brandeis and he was in
court to battle for Oregon's minimum hours law for women. It was

like Brandeis to champion an almost hopeless cause. Again and again he had taken time from a lucrative practice to fight for his dream of a "living law" that would reflect the needs of the twentieth century.

Brandeis knew he could not win his case with legal logic. The Lochner decision showed that. He decided on a bold new tack. He would fight with facts!

With reams of statistics he conjured up before the Court the picture of pale, overworked women, women succumbing to disease, women unable to bear healthy children and women unable to keep up their homes. He called on the justices to act as champions of the weaker sex. Uphold the Oregon law as a health measure, he argued.

Surprisingly, this novel approach worked. The Oregon law was upheld. More important, the Court's decision preserved similar laws in other states, and a new type of Supreme Court argument was born. An attorney's written argument is called his brief. To this day, when a brief relies more on the facts than on the legal technicalities, it is called a "Brandeis brief."

Holmes was delighted. He was one of Brandeis' most sincere admirers. They had taught together at Harvard University, and in those days had enjoyed many pleasant hours chatting over a snack in a Boston hotel. Now Brandeis was a welcome caller at Holmes' red brick house on I Street in Washington. The two men sat over the tea table in Holmes's book-lined parlor and eagerly thrashed out the affairs of the day. When Brandeis left, Holmes told his wife, Fanny, "There goes a really good man."

The "really good man" had won a really great victory. This, though, was only the beginning of a hard fight fraught with many setbacks for living law. After women won the vote in 1920 the justices decided that the weaker sex needed no more special protection, and in 1923, in the fateful case of *Adkins v. Children's Hospital,* the justices voided a women's minimum wage law, with Holmes, of course, dissenting.

Meanwhile, an exciting step toward liberalizing the Court was taken. On January 28, 1916, President Woodrow Wilson asked the Senate to confirm the appointment of Louis Brandeis to the Supreme Court. To Holmes, here at last was a chance to have an ally seated next to him on the bench. He knew the Court needed Brandeis if it was to understand the new issues of the time. The big question was, would a business-conscious Senate confirm this appointment? It irritated Holmes that the proceedings in the Senate committee room were dragging out interminably but, as a Supreme Court justice, he knew he must not appear to be trying to influence the legislative branch of the Government. He must not act. He could only sit out the winter in agonized silence waiting to see how his friend would fare. It was June 1 before the whole Senate took the final and decisive vote. At last, by a count of 47 to 22, Brandeis' nomination was confirmed.

Four days later, on June 5th, Louis D. Brandeis—the first Jew to be appointed to the Supreme Court—marched behind the other robed justices into the marble-pillared courtroom, and before a chamber packed with dignitaries from Congress, he took the oath of office and seated himself upon the bench. From that moment on, there were two great dissenters among the Supreme Court justices.

It was a fateful time in history for Brandeis to come to the bench. His liberal voice was about to be badly needed. Three months after he was appointed, the Congress passed the long-awaited child labor act forbidding goods made by children under fourteen from being shipped in interstate commerce. The bill was the result of more than a decade of lobbying by heartsick men and women moved by the sight of small children dragging heavy baskets and picking cotton in sun-drenched fields, or coughing their lungs out in the dusty mines collecting slate, or cooped up in damp lofts canning shrimp for ten and twelve hours a day. Children, they pleaded, should be in schools and playgrounds. In spite of all their pleas, within two years after their hard-fought-for act was passed it was being challenged before the Supreme Court. The test case was called *Hammer v. Dagenhart*.

Roland Dagenhart sent his two young sons, John, twelve, and Reuben, nine, to work each morning in a North Carolina cotton mill. There, in a dingy, lint-filled room crowded with humming spinning machines, Reuben, who weighed only sixty-five pounds, was made to lift and drag out bags of cotton weighing a hundred pounds. He worked twelve hours a day to earn one dollar. Years later he complained, "I had to leave school after the third grade, and now I need the education I didn't get."

When the new child labor law came into effect the manager told Dagenhart that the mill would have to dismiss the boys. The indignant parent, backed by various mill owners, decided to make his a test case. He brought his suit against W. C. Hammer, United States Attorney for the North Carolina area.

With an air of righteous indignation, Dagenhart's attorney asked the High Court, "Has Congress absorbed the police power of the state?" Whether or not a child worked in a mill was no affair of the Federal government, he maintained. It had nothing to do with interstate commerce. The goods transported across the state line were the same whether youngsters made them or not.

In vain the Solicitor General of the United States pointed out the evils of child labor—increased factory accidents, the stunted growth of the young, the pressure on other states to compete against the cheap, child-made goods.

Justice Day delivered the Court's opinion. "That there should be limitations upon the right to employ children in mines and factories in the interest of their own and the public welfare, all will admit," he said. But the Court was not ready yet to give Congress this much power over the lives of individuals engaged in commerce. Day insisted that child labor was solely a local and not an interstate responsibility. The law, therefore, was unconstitutional.

Now Holmes needed all he moral support he could get. His dissent had to be so ringing, so forceful, so sure, that this case could not and would not be the end of the matter.

"The statute," he said, "confines itself to prohibiting the carriage of certain goods in interstate or foreign commerce. Congress is given power to regulate such commerce in unqualified terms. . . . It does not matter whether the supposed evil precedes or follows the transportation [of goods]. It is enough that in the opinion of Congress the transportation encourages the evil. . . ."

These were the words of an angry man. In his anger Holmes was supported by Justices Brandeis, McKenna and Clarke, making this a close, five-to-four decision. The issue, as Holmes hoped, would come up again.

By now, old Chief Justice Fuller had been succeeded by Chief Justice Edward White; and when White died in 1921, President Warren G. Harding appointed ex-President William Howard Taft to the position. The two dissenters almost drove Taft out of his mind. Taft was a good-natured man. He liked both Holmes and Brandeis personally, but he hated the spectacle of a divided Court. There was more authority and impact in a unanimous decision. Taft wanted the voice of the Court to thunder with that authority.

Actually, the two men concurred with their colleagues much more often than they dissented, but it was their dissents that were conspicuous. Brandeis objected when the Court upheld an employer's right to get an injunction against a union organizer. It was no more coercion to call a strike than it was coercion to refuse to hire a man if he joined the union, he believed. Brandeis objected again when stone cutters in Denver, Colorado, organized a work stoppage on a building because they refused to carve or set limestone cut by nonunion men and the Court called this a conspiracy in restraint of trade. If the men weren't entitled to quit in numbers as well as individually they were being subjected to involuntary servitude. In other words, they were being treated like slaves. Holmes so frequently joined Brandeis in these dissents that at last Taft said of the old gentleman, "He is so completely under the control of brother Brandeis that it gives to Brandeis two votes instead of one."

This was not fair. The two friends were constant companions. They strolled together through the Washington streets; they shared a car to take a drive through the wooded Virginia hills; but, though they constantly conferred, they reached their conclusions from vastly different viewpoints. Holmes was skeptical of many of the new trends but thought the Constitution should not be a strait jacket to prevent them. Brandeis embodied the spirit of the new trends. He wanted the law to come alive and deal with the problems of this new era. He was anxious. If the law did not change to meet the times, something worse might happen. The advocates of some unwholesome theory or ism might one day take charge of the people.

Holmes was calmer. He had faith in the future. The legal needs of the working man would one day be met. He believed this as he worked for it. But as more years passed he grew tired of working.

In his late eighties he tired and grew drowsy during the long afternoon arguments heard by the Court. In 1932, at the age of 91, he retired, and three years later he went to his final rest. He did not live to see his dissents made the law of the land. It was up to the men who came after him to do that. It was up to Brandeis and other younger justices to turn Holmes' dissents into majority opinions. But this they did not do until after they were faced with a devastating national crisis and the fury of another great leader.

☆

"Proper Subject for Condemnation"

It was during the winter of 1936 that the papers in the crucial minimum wage law case, *West Coast Hotel Company v. Parrish,* reached the justices as they sat in their beautiful new white marble Court building. Then the eyes of the nation were on the Court. The drama in the suit was not only the fate of Elsie Parrish, who wanted the hotel company to pay her the minimum legal wage set by the State of Washington. Most of the suspense in the case was caused by the atmosphere in which it had to be decided.

There could hardly have been a worse moment in history for the justices to be asked to rule on a wage case. The Court was deep in a struggle with President Franklin Delano Roosevelt over labor legislation.

The state of the nation and the Court's fight with the President were more vital factors in Elsie Parrish's cause than Elsie herself. The President, who felt he was thwarted by the Court, was trying to cure the depression that had gripped the nation since the stock market crash of 1929.

At one point one out of every four family heads had been out of work. Local relief funds had given out. The unemployed queued up to stand for hours on city streets in wind and sleet just to wait for a bowl of soup. Citizens who had been evicted from their homes because they could not pay their rent broke into condemned buildings to escape the cold. As men grew more desperate, stores were broken into and farmers with pitchforks blocked the sheriff when he came to take their homesteads for the banks.

Part of the trouble was that those who were still employed worked for such low wages that they couldn't manage to live decently and didn't have the purchasing power to keep the remaining stores, farms and factories going. Among the lowest paid were hotel employees like Elsie Parrish.

By the time President Roosevelt mounted the inaugural platform on March 4, 1933, matters had grown worse. Bank failures in Michigan had precipitated a national hysteria. All over the land people were running to their own banks to draw out their funds, and the banks—the last bulwarks of the economic system—were collapsing.

The next day, Sunday, Roosevelt had closed the nation's banks for a week and halted the hysterical withdrawls. After that, for a hundred hectic days, the President had rushed emergency legislation from the White House to the Capitol, and a frightened "rubber stamp" Congress had passed all the bills he wanted in record time without worrying about whether the Court would uphold their constitutionality. Senator Carter Glass commented, "If the President asked Congress to commit suicide tomorrow they'd do it."

Actually, the American people were as impressed with Roosevelt as Congress was. Being crippled by polio and confined to a wheel chair had not kept this energetic man from campaigning his way to the Presidency or from tackling the national disaster almost single-handed. Accustomed to getting his own way, Roosevelt was not in the least prepared to take gracefully the setback he now faced at the hands of the Court.

It was late in 1934 when some of the President's hastily conceived legislation began coming before the justices. On May 27, 1935, after due deliberation, they threw out three of the President's programs, the most important of which was the National Industrial Recovery Act. This was also the one over which the President felt the most bitterness. The test case before the Court involved the Schechter Brothers, who were chicken dealers in Brooklyn, New York. The justices decided that they were not in interstate commerce and therefore not subject to Federal regulation. This narrow view of interstate commerce the Court was later to broaden. But the case of the National Industrial Recovery Act involved another vital issue. The lawmakers had simply delegated their lawmaking power to the Chief Executive because he asked for it, without setting guides as to how the power was to be used.

Actually, despite what happened next, Congress never again gave lawmaking power to the Executive branch of the government without first stating under what standards and limitations the laws were to be exercised.

That afternoon a presidential aide rushed to the White House to tell Roosevelt of the Court's decision, and the irate President immediately called a press conference. Two hundred reporters squeezed into his office at ten o'clock the next morning. He nodded them a grim greeting, put a cigarette in his holder and began to chat with a self-imposed nonchalance.

The Court's decision deprived him of all control over the economy, he complained. He characterized the justices as living in the "horse and buggy days." He wound up by assuring the press that something was going to be done about this.

But what? the reporters wanted to know. Was Roosevelt thinking of amending the Constitution? For the first time all morning, the President laughed. He was not telling yet what he intended doing.

For a while nothing more happened. Then, immediately after his overwhelming reelection in 1936, the storm broke. By that time the Court had thrown out more of the President's program. On February 6, 1937, Americans blinked at the headlines in their papers. Roosevelt wanted to change the structure of the Court. For every justice over seventy who would not retire he wanted to appoint an additional younger man. The justices would then number fifteen, six of whom would be of Roosevelt's own choosing. The Court, the President insisted, had so much work to do that the old gentlemen could not keep up with it. They were behind in their calendar. They needed young helpers.

As soon as this news broke, an alert *New York Times* reporter hastened to the Capitol steps, where he stopped various senators and asked their opinions of the President's proposal.

"A most ostentatious request for power," said Austin of Vermont.

"I most emphatically do not agree to packing the Supreme Court," said Vandenberg of Michigan.

Was the President's hypnotic charm losing its grip? Not entirely. There were those who said, "I am in favor."

Nevertheless, it was evident from the President's mail that the American people were not taking lightly his attempts to control the Court. This time many of them felt Roosevelt had gone too far, and they wrote and told him so. If any President could pack the Court to get his own way, the Court would no longer stand as a bulwark of liberty and a wall against the infringement of constitutional rights.

In the hope of getting the angered populace to change its mind, Roosevelt had three national broadcasting systems set up microphones in his White House office. In a dramatic effort to push his Court plan he gave one of his famous "fireside chats" over the radio.

He reminded the people of the dark days, of the hunger, poverty and want he had helped them survive. He asked them to trust him. He insisted it was the Court that had gone too far in throwing out legislation. "The Court has been acting not as a judicial body but as a policy-making body," he complained. Lastly, he promised the people he would not put spineless puppets on the bench. It was indeed a moving speech.

Meanwhile, Senators Wheeler, King and Austin had formed a committee to save the Court. Wheeler called on Brandeis in his office and Brandeis led his visitor straight to a telephone. "Call Hughes," he said. Wheeler did. Would the Chief Justice, he asked, appear before the senators who were considering the President's proposal and explain that the Court was not behind in its calendar?

Hughes wanted to go before Congress and to take Brandeis with him. Brandeis was then over seventy but such a highly regarded liberal that no one could claim he needed a more up-to-date mind to guide him. It was Brandeis, though, who dissuaded the Chief Justice from putting himself in the position of pleading before the senators.

Should he write a letter to defend the Court and show that it was up in its work, Hughes wanted to know? Brandeis agreed that he should.

Wheeler called for this letter at Hughes' home on Sunday, March 21, 1937. Standing in his own parlor, Hughes told the Senator, "If this bill should pass, it would destroy the Court as an institution." Wheeler agreed. He took the Chief Justice's message to present to the deeply divided, though largely pro-Roosevelt Senate committee.

While the senators considered this new evidence in the controversy, the justices gathered in their conference room to decide the crucial issue. How should they rule in *West Coast Hotel Company v. Parrish?* By now they had heard the arguments on both sides and knew all the facts.

In 1935 Elsie had been working for the hotel as a chambermaid. One gloomy day in May she dusted the bureaus, tucked in the bed sheets and then went down to see the manager. Jobs were scarce and Elsie was being discharged. It was then that the argument started.

The girl figured that the management had been cheating her all along. The Washington State Industrial Welfare Commission said employers had to pay women at least thirty-five cents an hour, or

$14.50 a week. Elsie had been getting only twenty-five cents an hour, which came to little more than ten dollars a week. Even the Welfare Commission statistics showed that that was not a living wage. Now that she was losing her job, Elsie at least found the courage to complain. She told the manager that he owed her $216.19 and should pay it. The manager refused.

Then Elsie and her husband, Ernest Parrish, went to see a lawyer, C. B. Conner, who helped them hale the West Coast Hotel Company into court. It was October 17 before the city trial court heard the case without a jury. The hotel company's attorney insisted that the Washington minimum wage law was unconstitutional and the court agreed. Elsie and Ernest indignantly appealed. Conner fought out the whole issue over again before the State Supreme Court of Washington in April, 1936. This time he won and the court said the hotel was compelled to pay the legal minimum wage. This time it was the hotel that was dissatisfied with the ruling.

It was therefore the hotel that had brought the case before the United States Supreme Court, relying on the Adkins decision, in which the Court had voided a minimum wage law for women. They relied also on the fact that four of the justices who had ruled in the Adkins case, Willis Van Devanter, James C. McReynolds, George Sutherland and Pierce Butler, were still there and could be counted on to rule again that a wage law violated the rights of adults to make their own contracts.

There were, however, four other justices in the conference room whose attitudes were quite different. One of these was Chief Justice Charles Evans Hughes, a tall man with an erect posture, whose beard and moustache partly covered his long, oval face. He had been a liberal Governor of New York, a narrowly defeated Presidential candidate in 1916, and Secretary of State under Presidents Harding and Coolidge.

Then there was Associate Justice Harlan Stone to consider. In the past, Stone had often sided with "those two," Holmes and Brandeis. Now that Holmes was gone, Brandeis had Stone and Benjamin N. Cardozo to keep him company. Cardozo was "that Democrat from New York" appointed by Hoover to replace Holmes. Cardozo, so people said, was doing his best to be as liberal as his predecessor.

Elsie and her attorney could expect Hughes, Stone, Brandeis and Cardozo to vote in her favor.

The decision would then turn on the vote of the Mystery Judge —Owen Roberts. Nobody ever knew where Roberts stood until a case was over. Edwin Corwin, who writing about the Court in his book *Constitutional Revolution, Ltd.*, said that after a challenging case Roberts paced the floor of his Washington house until all hours of the night trying to decide where he stood.

With the Court so bitterly divided, Hughes had a hard time leading the discussion and keeping it orderly. As was expected by the litigants, Van Devanter, McReynolds, Sutherland and Butler wanted to throw out the state law; Hughes, Stone, Brandeis and Cardozo wanted to uphold the state. The trouble was that neither the four conservatives nor the four liberals could swing the Court without Roberts. Justice Roberts had to make up his mind.

With the Court's own existence hanging in the balance, Roberts weighed the question. Should the Court uphold the state law? Observers noted that if the law should be thrown out, the Court would be taking another slap at Roosevelt's economic program. On the other hand, a decision upholding the state statute would be inconsistent with the Court's position in *Adkins v. Children's Hospital*.

While the justices were discussing the case, Hughes quoted Holmes' dissent in the Adkins case. Possibly it moved Roberts as it obviously had Hughes. There were those who said Roberts was influenced by Roosevelt's Court reorganization threat. Others vigorously denied it. In any case, this time Roberts swung the balance to the liberal wing and the minimum wage law was upheld. Elsie Parrish won her $14.50 a week and state minimum wage laws survived, but something even more important was achieved. Decisions like this made the work of the senators who were defending the Court a lot easier. Through their efforts the Court reoganization bill eventually failed. The judiciary, as an independent institution, was preserved.

Meanwhile, less than a month after the Parrish decision, the liberal wing of the Court, with Roberts' help, was in a position to announce that "acts which directly burden or obstruct interstate or foreign commerce, or its free flow, are within the reach of congressional power"—including acts having that effect which "grow out of labor disputes." Further, the Court said, employees in industry have a "fundamental right" to organize and select representatives of their own choosing for collective bargaining. "Discrimination and coercion [upon the part of the employers] to prevent the free exercise of the right . . . is a proper subject for condemnation by competent legislative authority." In other words, Congress had the power to prevent any person from engaging in unfair labor practices affecting commerce.

That case was called the *National Labor Relations Board v. Jones and Laughlin Steel Corporation.* How Holmes would have loved it! At last both state and Federal government could protect labor unions and prescribe minimum wage laws.

That same year, conservative Associate Justice Van Devanter resigned and Roosevelt was able to appoint Hugo Black, giving the Court a liberal majority of five without packing or destroying it. Now Brandeis was no longer the Great Dissenter but the leader of the majority. He had lived to see his views become the law.

Later, more changes that he and Holmes had wanted came about. Although Brandeis was no longer on the bench in 1941 when the Court overruled its own stand against Federal child labor laws in a case called *United States v. Darby,* he was still alive to know about it and to think how happy Holmes would have been.

Stone, who had been promoted to Chief Justice, read the Court's opinion in this case. In declaring the power of Congress to legislate against child labor and to prevent goods made by children from being shipped in interstate commerce, the Chief Justice quoted Holmes' dissent in the Dagenhart case. Justice Holmes would not have been surprised. The old soldier had at last triumphed with his great opinions, just as he always expected to when he was patiently writing them.

In addition, Congress passed new and more careful laws to carry out Roosevelt's program and to replace the legislation the Court would not permit. Laws to regulate industry and help farmers and workers were put on the books, and once again America had come through a challenge brought on by the new economic age with her free institutions intact.

Bibliography
Principal Sources, Case 7

BOOKS

Biddle, Francis, *Mr. Justice Holmes.* New York. 1943.
Bowen, Catherine Drinker, *Yankee from Olympus.* Boston. 1944.
Frankfurter, Felix (editor), *Mr. Justice Brandeis.* Yale. 1932.

Mason, Alpheus Thomas, *Brandeis, A Free Man's Life*. New York. 1946.

Pringle, Henry F., *The Life and Times of William Howard Taft*. New York. 1939.

Pusey, Merlo John, *Charles Evans Hughes*. New York. 1951.

Schlesinger, Arthur M., Jr., *The Crisis of The Old Order*. Boston. 1957.

UNITED STATES FEDERAL RECORDS

Adkins v. Children's Hospital, 261 U.S. 525 (1923).

Adair v. United States, 208 U.S. 161 (1908).

Bedford Cut Stone v. Journeymen Cutters' Ass'n., 274 U.S. 37 (1927).

Coppage v. Kansas, 236 U.S. 1 (1915).

Hammer v. Dagenhart, 247 U.S. 251 (1918).

Lochner v. New York, 198 U.S. 45 (1905).

Muller v. Oregon, 208 U.S. 412 (1908).

Schechter Poultry Corporation v. United States, 295 U.S. 495 (1935).

National Labor Relations Board v. Jones and Laughlin Steel Corp., 301 U.S. 1 (1937).

West Coast Hotel Company v. Parrish, 300 U.S. 379 (1937).

NEWSPAPERS

New York Times, June 6, 1916, June 15, 1935, February 6, 1937, March 9, 1937.

New York Tribune, May 22, 1936.

MAGAZINE ARTICLES

Abbot, Grace, "Regulation of Child Labor." *Social Service Review* (Sept. 1939).

Brandeis, Louis D., "The Living Law." *Illinois Law Review*, Vol. 10 (Feb. 1916).

Padway, Joseph, "Brandeis and Labor." *American Federationist* (Dec. 1941).

"To Justice Oliver Wendell Holmes" (excerpts from his speeches). *Illinois Law Review*, Vol. 10 (Apr. 1916).

☆ CASE 8 ☆

Brown v. *Board of Education*

The Court Orders Public Schools
to Integrate

---

*"In approaching this problem, we cannot turn
the clock back . . ."*

EARL WARREN, 1954

THE TIMES
AND THE ISSUES

After January 1, 1863, by virtue of Abraham Lincoln's famous Emancipation Proclamation, the Southern slaves were declared to be "thenceforward and forever free." Congress attempted to put the Proclamation into effect for all Negroes by framing and sending to the states for ratification the Thirteenth, Fourteenth and Fifteenth Amendments. The Thirteenth abolished slavery. The Fourteenth guaranteed the Negro citizenship. Further, the Fourteenth forced the states to grant to all men the equal protection of the laws, and even more, protection from being deprived of life, liberty, or property without due process of law. The Fifteenth guaranteed a citizen's voting rights.

The President's proclamation was a wartime act, and the amendments framed by Congress were acts of victory thrust on the vanquished while they were still under military occupation. In fact, no Confederate state could be readmitted into the Union until it had adopted the Fourteenth Amendment. Acts born of war and victory are likely to be resisted by the vanquished. And so they were.

Well-meaning persons wanting to see peace and harmony throughout the land begged the Negro to assert his rights gradually. But by the beginning of the nineteen fifties educated Negroes were insisting that a hundred years was gradual enough. They turned to the Supreme Court to make the promises in the Emancipation Proclamation and the Constitution come true.

Included in their most dramatic battles were the school desegregation cases that they brought before the Court. There were five of these cases. Only later were they all referred to by the name of one of their number, *Brown v. The Board of Education of Topeka.*

"I Am Not Authorized to Enroll You"

Five roads led to the Supreme Court as five different Negro groups in five different parts of the country, determined to achieve equality, picked school desegregation as the most important channel for their energies. Their meetings were permeated with excitement and determination. Here was one of the sources responsible for those attitudes that deprived Negroes of a fair and equal chance to get ahead and hold good positions in the community. Sending children to separate schools, they reasoned, tended to teach the white youngsters that Negroes were people to be excluded. Prejudice on the part of individuals was bad enough, they declared, but school segregation constituted government-enforced discrimination. Here, then, was one place to strike at racial injustice.

Significantly, one of the earliest episodes in the integration struggle took place in Washington, D.C., the nation's capital. It started on Monday, September 11, 1950. Spottswood Bolling, a Negro teenager, his brother Wanamaker, and their mother waited anxiously on a sunny street corner in front of a church. With them were Mrs. James C. Jennings, her two daughters, Adrienne and Barbara, and a young friend, Sarah Briscoe.

Several cars pulled up to the curb. With grim determination Spottswood followed his mother and brother into one of them. He was a thin, shy boy and the experience he faced this morning was particularly difficult for him. The cars were driving to Sousa Junior High, an all-white school. There the young people expected to be put through the indignity of being refused admission because they were colored. But the step had to be taken.

The little group was making the first necessary move in a legal battle to end segregation in public schools. They were out to make social history. Going with the boys and girls and their parents were, among others, a Negro pastor and Gardner Bishop, the President of a Negro civic society called the Consolidated Parents League.

What a way to go to school! If Spottswood could have hidden

under the car seat he would have done so rather than be this conspicuous. Perhaps the others were excited by the adventure; certainly they were indignant at the necessity for it.

Mrs. Jennings, the mother of two of the girls, stated her own reason for feeling rebellious. It cost her three dollars a week, she said, to send her five children to Negro schools when Sousa was within walking distance. She was tired of being shunted around, and her family could ill afford the expense.

Mrs. Bolling was more outraged than Mrs. Jennings. Spottswood and Wanamaker had been assigned to the old Birney school building, where water leaked into the auditorium. "I didn't want them to go to that pig pen," she complained. "They'd been brought up in a very clean home."

Sousa Junior High School was a beautiful, inviting, new red brick building with big windows.

To Mr. Bishop, the newness of the building or its closeness to the Jennings home was not the point. Segregating children of the same age on the basis of their color was undemocratic and humiliating for the minority being pushed aside. He thought it was time to tell the world that this practice was not in keeping with the principles of the United States Constitution.

According to one newspaper reporter, as they got out of their cars and walked past a group of sneering Sousa parents they were told, "You know you're going to lose."

The Negroes said nothing, but walked quietly to a side door, entered the building and marched resolutely down the hall to the office of the principal, Miss Eleanor P. McAuliffe. She was sorry, the small woman told the children in a dignified tone, "but I am not authorized to enroll you." Her manner indicated that there was nothing for them to do but leave her school.

The determined little group next drove downtown to the school system's administration building. There, the superintendent of schools, a tall, emaciated-looking older man, told them in an offended tone that under the law Negroes could not be admitted to white schools.

All this they had expected. Spottswood and the others went back to their own school. The grownups appealed to the Board of Education to end segregation. Plenty of Washingtonians agreed with them, urging that it was a disgrace to discriminate against people on the basis of race, especially in the capital of the world's foremost democracy. The Board backed the superintendent. Congress had given them appropriations for two sets of schools, they said.

The Negroes next took the step that they had anticipated would be necessary all along. They went into the Federal court. Judge Walter M. Bastian was very sorry, but he felt compelled to dismiss their case.

Under the law, Negro schools had to be made equal to white schools. But that was not what the Consolidated Parents League was asking for. Through their lawyers, George E. C. Hayes and Dr. James M. Nabrit, they were calling for a social revolution—an end to segregation. On that score the judge considered himself bound by a Supreme Court ruling handed down in 1896 in a case called *Plessy v. Ferguson*. The lawyers, of course, were unpleasantly aware of that case.

Years back, Homer Adolph Plessy had bought a ticket on a Louisiana railroad from New Orleans to Covington. Plessy, who was part Negro, took a seat in the white coach. He was asked to move. He refused, and was sent to jail in New Orleans. When the case came up before the Supreme Court the justices had ruled that "[Segregated facilities] do not necessarily imply the inferiority of either race to the other, and have been generally, if not universally, recognized as within the competency of state legislatures in the exercise of their police power. The most common instance of this is connected with the establishment of separate schools." All that the law required, the Court had said, was that the facilities provided for one race be equal to those provided for the other. The one dissenting justice, John Marshall Harlan, made his now famous remark, "Our Constitution is color blind."

Since the *Plessy* decision, school systems in the South and border states had taken the position that "separate but equal" school systems for whites and Negroes were legal. At the time of Spottswood's historic ride to Sousa Junior High, seventeen states had laws requiring segregation in their schools and that was what the Parents League was determined to eradicate. Undaunted by losing their case before Judge Bastian, the Negroes went to work and raised money to bring the cause before the highest Court in the land.

They were not to be alone. They were to have plenty of support. Everywhere Negro communities were in a state of turmoil. Everywhere, Negro leaders wanted to eradicate the demeaning concept that separate but equal was good enough for their people. All over the land other integration groups were either already started or about to get under way.

It was a mere seven months after Spottswood's visit to Sousa that the telephone rang in the Richmond law office of Oliver W. Hill, an attorney for the National Association for the Advancement of Colored People. A group of Negro high school Seniors in Virginia's Prince Edward County, seventy miles away, were geared for action. They were going out on strike against their school. For years the Negro young people had been attending classes in makeshift tarpaper shacks. The main colored high school building had been overcrowded since the day it opened. Constructing tarpaper shacks was the county's way of handling the situation. The flimsy structures were heated by stove pipes that led out from an oil drum. Obviously they were a fire hazard.

Attorney Hill's caller was a girl named Barbara Johns. Barbara, a bright, active teen-ager and a class leader, had grown up in a family that had been protesting these bad safety conditions at public meetings and before public officials for more than ten years. Enthusiastically she argued that if her idea worked and the strike made the county build a new high school, the new school would be her crowd's gift to the younger students she would be leaving behind when she graduated.

Could Hill help her? she asked. A friendly, communicative advocate, Hill agreed to come and talk to the young people's parents. To them, he explained that trying to get the county to improve conditions in Negro schools was not the answer. The only solution, he felt, was to end segregation. The year before, he said, South Carolina parents had started a suit to that end. Virginia P.T.A. groups should do the same.

Exactly one month later the Virginia Negro parents from Prince Edward County went into Federal court, and as the South Carolina parent group had done, they pleaded with the court to end segregation. Both sets of parents cited the neglect of school buildings and curriculum. The only way to insure that colored people received as good an education as whites, they insisted, was to have the two races go to school together.

In both the Virginia and the South Carolina cases the United States district courts dealt with the problem by finding the provisions made for Negro schools inferior to those made for white

schools and ordering the school boards to begin immediately to
equalize the facilities. That left the Negro children in admittedly
inferior physical surroundings until something was done—and as
the Negroes saw it, based on past experience, the equalizing, even if
it took place, would be only temporary. As the Parents League had
done, the Virginia and South Carolina groups went ahead with their
own plans to appeal to the United States Supreme Court.

The now-famous Brown case began in 1952. The Reverend
Oliver Brown lived four blocks from the all-white Sumner Ele-
mentary School of Topeka, Kansas. His plump little eight-year-old
daughter, Linda, played all summer long with the children of her
white neighbors, but when registration started at the Sumner School
the principal refused to register Linda. Kansas law permitted segregation and Topeka chose to have it.

The minister, a mild, quiet man, was pained at the thought that
bigotry and discrimination would always stand in his child's way.
"She seems very apt," he said. "I want her to have something more
to look forward to than washing dishes."

He couldn't know it then, but one day Linda, who was not only
bright but also musical, would win a scholarship to college. Meanwhile her parents were worried about her future and distressed at
the spectacle of her growing up in a segregated school system. They
were distressed, too, at her having to cross a dangerous railroad
bridge and stand in the rain waiting for a badly overcrowded school
bus to carry her twenty blocks away when Sumner was only a
short walk from their door. Her father called a friend at the National Association for the Advancement of Colored People, to
discuss the matter. Then, with some other Negro parents, the Browns
decided to challenge the system in the United States District Court
for the District of Kansas.

Like many advocates of civil rights everywhere, these people
knew that segregation made the Negro child feel that no matter
how good he was or how hard he tried he would always be somebody to be cast aside. The very thought could break a youngster's
morale and block his development. Separate schools were in-
herently unfair. Depriving a Negro of equal status in the community was subjecting him to a kind of bondage—the bondage of
second-class citizenship. Negroes had a right to be free.

Kansas was not a center of intense racial conflict. Many schools in the state were already integrated. The three judges of the District Court sympathetically wrote into the record that segregation in public education did, in truth, have a detrimental effect on Negro children. But then the judges refused to rule against it. They pointed out that Negro and white schools in Topeka were equal as to buildings, educational qualifications of teachers, and so forth. Therefore, like Judge Bastian, they felt bound by the Plessy decision of more than half a century before. There seemed no help for the Negro dream of attacking prejudice born of ignorance and perpetuated by the existence of segregated schools unless the Supreme Court of the United States could be persuaded to reverse its earlier position. That is something the Court is reluctant to do. Both the Court and the country like the law to be predictable and reliable.

In the face of this discouraging obstacle, the Reverend Oliver Brown patiently undertook to lead his flock to back his case and bring it, along with the others, before the highest Court in the land.

Meanwhile, there had been an interesting case in Delaware. Negro parents there had not taken their problem into the Federal court. Instead, they had gone before the Delaware Court of Chancery. Conditions in Delaware were not as bad as in Prince Edward County, Virginia, but they were bad enough. The makeshift cafeteria in one Wilmington high school for Negroes was so small that students had to stand to eat their lunch. The building had no auditorium for assemblies and no grounds around it that could be used for a physical education program.

Besides, the Delaware parents argued, as had the Reverend Oliver Brown, segregation itself was bad. Reference was made to the psychological effect on white as well as Negro students. And Delaware Negroes were not alone in dreaming of the day when white students would no longer meet only colored people who were menials and never know a colored family where the father was a teacher, a lawyer, a doctor, or a scientist.

Attorney General Albert Young countered the Negro request by calling experts to testify that the population had to be educated slowly before it could be peaceably induced to give up such an old Southern custom as segregation. It was obvious to the colored people, however, that the longer the custom lasted the more entrenched it became.

The Chancellor surprised everyone. Without ruling on the principle of segregation, which he nevertheless said resulted in an inferior education for Negro children, he ordered the white schools to admit Negroes. The buildings available to colored students were not nearly as good as those provided for white students. Therefore, said the Chancellor, the state was violating the Fourteenth Amendment to the Constitution: ". . . nor shall any State . . . deny to any person within its jurisdiction the equal protection of the laws." More surprising, the Supreme Court of Delaware upheld the Chancellor but intimated that the order was to last only until facilities for Negroes were improved.

Delaware's Attorney General asked the justices of the United States Supreme Court to review the findings of his State Court and they agreed to hear his arguments. Now there were five cases on segregation pending before the Court.

The excited Negroes and their friends were not the only ones anxiously waiting to see how the Supreme Court would react to their plea. Devoted civil servants in the United States State Department waited with equal concern. To them the shabby treatment of the American Negro was a nightmare situation, sabotaging their efforts to keep the uncommitted colored peoples of Asia and Africa friendly to the United States and out of the Communist camp.

Southern whites waited anxiously, too, but their position was different. As they saw it, their whole way of life, based as it was on a belief in white supremacy, was threatened. Many of them stated flatly that they would preserve their customs at all costs. Thus, by the time the Court met, tension and turbulence smouldered on all sides.

☆

"With All Deliberate Speed"

December 9, 1952! Outside, it was raining; inside the marble and mahogany courtroom in the Supreme Court building, the thickset, wavy-haired Negro attorney stood before the bench and in an earnest, low voice showered the justices with arguments against the segregation of school children. The lawyer was Thurgood Marshall, who had won more civil rights cases than anyone cared to count. He was a true giant of the American bar, and his own spirits were not dampened either by the weather or by the fact that four of the justices listening to him came from states that maintained school segregation.

Short and slight, Associate Justice Black came from the heart of white supremacy territory—Alabama. But Marshall knew that Black took his Bill of Rights very literally. Chief Justice Fred M. Vinson, who, like Associate Justice Stanley Reed, came from segregated Kentucky, was known for his gentle, conciliatory nature, and so was Tom Clark, from segregated Texas. How far they would go in this tense hour, to break with old precedents and give a suppressed race a fairer chance, no one could tell. But one could hope. After all, in addition to Black and Reed, three other justices had been appointed by that humanitarian President Franklin Delano Roosevelt. One of them was William O. Douglas, known to love justice as he loved the great outdoors. Another was Robert Jackson, whose New York training would have led him away from discrimination. The third was Felix Frankfurter, who swiveled nervously in his high-backed leather chair and, as was his habit, snapped questions at the attorneys. Also on the bench were Sherman Minton of Indiana and Justice Harold H. Burton of Ohio, who made helpful leading comments.

For three whole days the justices listened to the first of a series of arguments in the "School Cases." The hearings were to drag out into 1955. One of the nine was destined never to hear the end of the debate. Chief Justice Vinson died in September, 1953. Thus, while the Court grappled with one of the biggest cases in its history and America's destiny hung in the balance, President Eisenhower was forced to look for someone who could replace Vinson and bring harmony to the bench. He chose the Governor of California, Earl Warren.

The new Chief Justice was a large, frank, likable man. His approach to law had always been as practical as it was theoretical. Time and again in the years ahead he would ask an arguing attorney, "Were you fair?"

To convince the justices of the worthiness of their cause the Negro lawyers worked as a team, helping with each other's written briefs and oral arguments. They presented the Brown case first.

Justice Burton listened and nodded, "There is a great deal more to the educational process than what you read in books," he commented.

Later, Burton directed a question at Kansas Attorney General Paul E. Wilson, who was arguing for school segregation. "Don't you recognize it as a possibility," the Justice asked, "that in seventy-five years the social and economic conditions of the nation have changed so that what might have been a valid interpretation of the Fourteenth Amendment seventy-five years ago would not be valid today?" His point is the heart of much constitutional interpretation.

Wilson answered it by saying that the *Plessy* decision, legalizing separate but equal facilities for whites and Negroes, was still the binding precedent in this area.

Justice Frankfurter then asked Wilson how serious the problems of the local school board would be if the Court ordered the desegregation of schools.

Wilson answered, "In perfect candor, I must say to the Court that the consequences would probably not be serious." The Negro population of Kansas was small, he noted, and Negro schools were on a par with the whites.

What, Frankfurter wanted to know, would happen in states where the Negro population was large?

Wilson said he couldn't speak for states other than Kansas.

Virginia's Attorney General Almond, when his turn came, felt it would be very disrupting to desegregate schools. It would be hard, in his state, he said, to float a school bond to raise money for integrated schools.

Almond was fully supported in his argument by John W. Davis, a suave, white-haired attorney representing South Carolina. Mr. Davis was a formidable foe for the Negro lawyers to battle. Well known as a successful advocate, he counted among his clients those who could afford the finest. In his argument, Davis stressed states' rights, but he argued also that tension might arise and trouble develop in the wake of desegregation in the South.

Thurgood Marshall answered, "The people of the South are not lawless." If desegregation should be ordered by the Court, he said, he thought they would obey. As for states' rights, the Court could still interpret the Constitution.

Slavery had been outlawed a long time ago but segregation was designed to keep the Negro people in as nearly that state as possible, he argued, and the psychological effects of this were fully covered in his written brief.

The child who accepts for himself the demeaning status of a segregated citizen does not develop his capacities, he maintained. The child who resents his inferior position in society may become aggressive. In either case, the educational experience of the Negroes—since education is all of what one learns—was not equal to the educational experience of the whites. The white child was learning to expect to enjoy the fruits of his achievements and to be appreciated for his abilities; the Negro was not, and the existence of segregated schools perpetuated this intolerable caste system.

In their separate offices the justices studied Marshall's words and recalled the oral statements. Months went by. Newspaper reporters following the proceedings refused to guess what the justices would do. It was June of 1953 before the justices said anything. Then they neither upheld the concept of separate but equal facilities nor ordered desegregation. Instead, they asked for more arguments by the attorneys.

Specifically, the Court wanted the attorneys to dwell on the law. What, they asked, was intended by those who framed the Fourteenth Amendment? Did the framers contemplate school desegregation? It is, after all, the function of the Court to say what the law is, not what might be desirable.

Furthermore, the Court had to determine whether, if it ordered the states to desegregate their schools, it could legally let them do it gradually. The justices were aware that in many communities building facilities were not adequate to permit immediate wholesale redistricting.

And finally, the justices asked for suggestions as to how, if they ruled that it was necessary, integration could be enforced.

These were complicated questions. The justices invited the Attorney General of the United States, Herbert Brownell, to participate in their consideration. It was December before all parties, including the Department of Justice, were ready to be heard.

Thurgood Marshall argued that the Fourteenth Amendment was intended to abolish all vestiges of a caste system in America. He quoted the statements of various senators and congressmen who had worked on framing the amendment. He was, in addition, against gradualism. The Negroes should be admitted to white schools at once, he said. Otherwise, Negroes were not getting their rights.

The lawyer representing the Attorney General agreed with Marshall that the Fourteenth Amendment was intended to express a broad and continuing program to establish full freedom and full and complete equality of all persons under the law. But the Department of Justice felt that, in the public interest, the Court should give the school systems the necessary time to adjust—to rearrange their facilities and prepare for integration. As for enforcing the Court's order, the Attorney General and his assistants in the Department of Justice felt that this could be left to the lower courts.

During his discussion of this last point the Government lawyer talked as if integration were imminent. Horrified, Davis made one more plea for states' rights. "Your honors do not sit, and cannot sit, as a glorified board of education for the State of South Carolina or any other state," he declared. "Neither can the district court."

Davis did not think it mattered that Thurgood Marshall could quote the opinions of individual senators and congressmen on the meaning of the Fourteenth Amendment. The point was, he said, that Congress had framed the amendment, and Congress maintained a segregated school system in Washington, D.C., itself.

This was a hard argument to answer, and when the justices arose and filed out behind the red felt curtain that backed the bench, the effects of Davis' words were still in the air.

By now the entire nation was following the proceedings before the high Court with the greatest fascination. Newspaper reporters, conscious of the demands of their readers, hurried to the Court building each Monday, the Court's traditional decision day. There, they waited impatiently in the press room. Each week they hoped that this was the time the big story would break.

Time after time they were disappointed. Many of them used the delay to prepare background material to print along with the great news when it finally came. But how would their articles end? They could be certain of only one thing. The justices would rule on a Monday, as they always did.

At last, on Monday, May 17, 1954, the Supreme Court Press Officer darted into the reporters' waiting room. With the air of a man trying to announce a fire calmly, he told the journalists, "Opinions on the school cases are about to be read in the Courtroom." The reporters followed him hurriedly through the marble halls into the Court Chamber and seated themselves on the pewlike red-cushioned seats. There was a tense hush as Chief Justice Warren slowly and clearly began to read the opinion of the unanimous Court.

The Chief Justice started by reviewing the background of four of the cases. Methodically, he reminded his listeners of how the Negroes had been denied admittance to white schools, of their fight in the lower courts and their final plea here before the Highest Court.

Then he went on to take up the big question: What did the framers of the Fourteenth Amendment have in mind as to school segregation when the amendment was adopted in 1868?

The Chief Justice spoke of all the sources cited by the attorneys during the argument and of all the sources the justices had uncovered during their own study. He decided they were all "inconclusive." The framers of the amendment had said comparatively little about schools. The Chief Justice was not surprised at this, and he explained why.

"In the South, [in 1868] the movement toward free common schools, supported by general taxation, had not yet taken hold. . . . Even in the North . . . the school term was but three months a year in many states." Consequently, the framers of the amendment had not given much consideration to schools. In the years since, the Chief Justice explained, the importance of formal education to success in life had grown enormously. This the Court had borne in mind. Also, through the years, Negroes had shown that they could qualify to enter the sciences and the professions if given the chance. At the same time the world had developed its knowledge of psychology and the psychological effects on individuals of discrimination.

"In approaching the problem," the Chief Justice reasoned, "we cannot turn the clock back to 1868 when the Amendment was adopted, or even to 1896 when *Plessy v. Ferguson* was written. We must consider public education in the light of its . . . present place in American life. . . . Today, education is perhaps the most important function of state and local governments. . . . It is the very foundation of good citizenship. . . . In these days, it is doubtful that any child may reasonably be expected to succeed in life if he is denied the opportunity of an education. Such an opportunity, where the state has undertaken to provide it, is a right which must be made available to all on equal terms.

"We come then to the question presented: Does segregation of children in public schools solely on the basis of race, even though the physical facilities and other 'tangible' factors may be equal, deprive the children of the minority group of equal educational opportunities? We believe that it does."

A reporter somewhere in the audience whispered, "That does it!" America, he felt sure, had taken the next big step toward realizing the ideal chiseled on the marble portal of that very building: "Equal justice under law."

Two major moves still had to be made before anything at all resulted from the Court's order. For one thing, the nation's capital had to set an example to the nation by integrating its schools. This required that the Court make a separate ruling in the Spottswood Bolling case. The other four cases had been decided on the basis of the Fourteenth Amendment, but Washington, D.C., is not a state and hence the Fourteenth Amendment did not apply to it.

The justices therefore examined what is known as the "due process" clause of the Fifth Amendment. "No person shall be deprived of life, liberty, or property, without due process of law." On the basis of this, the Court ruled that segregation in public schools "imposes on Negro children . . . a burden that constitutes an arbitrary deprivation of their liberty."

In addition, and even more vital, the Court had to turn its attention to getting its decision implemented. The justices wisely scheduled more hearings in order to determine how this should be done. By so doing they were consciously giving the Southern States time—a full year—to adjust to the shock of the decision. After that, it would somehow have to be enforced.

The exhausted attorneys went back to plan their final arguments on this all-important point. On May 31, 1955, the Court, in its final decision, placed on the lower courts the responsibility of seeing to it that all school boards made a prompt and reasonable start toward complying with the law, to the end that they implement the desegregation order "with all deliberate speed."

Spottswood Bolling's high school in Washington was integrated before he graduated. He won a scholarship to college and decided to major in physical education. In the District of Columbia, where he lived, integration was carried out quickly and easily. The people were ready for it. All they needed was a spark, an impetus, to make them act instead of endlessly talking about eventual integration.

The Board of Education of Linda Brown's Topeka, Kansas, school system voted to integrate even before the Supreme Court's final ruling. Like Spottswood, Linda also went to college on a scholarship. Thurgood Marshall, the attorney who had helped them all so much, was later made a Federal Appeals Court judge by President John F. Kennedy.

Meanwhile, in the country's border states desegregation progressed with reasonable smoothness. In Oklahoma, despite the southern population near its Texas border, integration was accomplished without great difficulty. Negroes had never had trouble voting in Oklahoma, and people who vote get consideration. There were, in addition, no elected demagogues to incite mob violence.

In Missouri, Kentucky, West Virginia, Maryland and Delaware, the Oklahoma story was more or less repeated. Flare-ups in only a few trouble spots made headlines in the papers.

In some deep southern states, unhappily, this was not the case. Passions erupted like an angry volcano. Howling mobs encircled school buildings, blocking the entrance of colored students. Negro young people lived in fear for their lives.

In other areas pupil placement laws were designed to maintain segregation. Compulsory school attendance statutes were repealed; schools were closed. In Prince Edward County, Virginia, a system of private schools was installed and the public schools were shut. For four years, until makeshift arrangements were made, Negroes went without schooling. Barbara Johns, the leader of the old school strike—now married to a social worker in Philadelphia—gasped in horror. Segregated schools would be better for Negroes than none, she told a reporter. The Negro parents in Prince Edward County did not agree. Instead of giving in, they went back through the courts, and in May of 1964 the Supreme Court had another ruling to make.

At this point the justices took a look at the nation's record. Since they had ruled ten years before, every state in the Union except Mississippi had achieved at least some token integration, but in many of the southern states it was negligible. Back in 1954 the justices had told the states to move "with all deliberate speed."

Now, on May 25, 1964, they told the nation, "The time for mere 'deliberate speed' has run out, and that phrase can no longer justify denying these Prince Edward County school children their constitutional rights to an education equal to that afforded by the public schools in other parts of Virginia."

Opposition to desegregation did not constitute a legal reason to close schools, they said. They ordered the public schools to reopen. By so doing they served notice on other school boards that the Court was getting impatient. It wanted compliance with its orders. Progress in the next decade must be speedier. And in the fall of 1964 Prince Edward County reopened its public schools.

Thus, the Negroes had won another battle, this one against evasion. More important, the school desegregation fight had served as a symbol. It encouraged colored people to stand up for their rights in other areas—to demand fair practices in transportation, housing and employment. Most important of all, the Negro knows he can rely on the forces of law to help him achieve the status he feels he must have. In spite of how little integration the deep South has achieved, the law of the land has changed, creating a new atmosphere toward the Negro cause. Since the decision of 1954, courts have outlawed segregation in parks, on beaches and in local transit systems. In 1964 Congress passed a strong civil rights act that bars discrimination in employment, and in hotels, restaurants and other public places.

Bibliography
Principal Sources, Case 8

BOOKS

Williams, Robin M., Jr., and Ryan, Margaret W., *Schools in Transition*. North Carolina. 1954.

UNITED STATES FEDERAL RECORDS—TRANSCRIPTS OF RECORDS AND COPIES OF THE BRIEFS

Bolling v. Sharpe, Docket No. 8, Oct. Term 1953. 347 U.S. 497.

Briggs v. Elliott, Docket No. 2, Oct. Term 1953. 347 U.S. 483.

Brown v. Board of Education of Topeka, Docket No. 1, Oct. Term 1953. 347 U.S. 483.

Davis v. County School Board of Prince Edward County, Docket
No. 4, Oct. Term 1953. 347 U.S. 483.

Gebhart v. Belton, Docket No. 10, Oct. Term 1953. 347 U.S. 483.

Plessy v. Ferguson, 163 U.S. 537.

NEWSPAPERS

New York Times, Feb. 12, 1961; May 18, 1954; June 21, 1964.

Washington Post, Sept. 29, 1963; May 17, 1964; May 26, 1964.

The Evening Star (Washington), Dec. 14, 1942; May 15, 17 and
25, 1964.

MAGAZINES

"A Historic Decision for Equality," *Life* (May 31, 1954).

"Arguments Before the Court," *United States Law Week* (Dec. 16,
1952).

Caliver, Ambrose, "Education of Negroes—Segregation issue before the Supreme Court." *School Life* (Feb. 1954).

Fitzpatrick, Edward A., "History of Non-Segregation and other
Racial and Judicial Decisions." *School Board Journal* (Aug.
1954).

Leflar, Robert A., and Davis, Wylie H., "Segregation in Public
Schools," *Harvard Law Review,* Vol. 67. (Jan. 1954).

"May It Please the Court." *Time* (Dec. 21, 1953).

Poling, James, "Thurgood Marshall and the Fourteenth Amendment." *Collier's* (Feb. 23, 1952). "The Warren Court." *News-
week* (May 11, 1964).

☆ CASE 9 ☆

School District of Abington Township v. Schempp

The Court Reinforces the Wall Separating Church and State

"If there is any principle of the Constitution that more imperatively calls for attachment than any other it is the principle of free thought—not free thought for those who agree with us but freedom for the thought we hate."

OLIVER WENDELL HOLMES, 1929

THE TIMES
AND THE ISSUES

Church and state were not separated in the Old World from which the American settlers came. To keep control over the minds of their subjects, Catholic monarchs ordered Protestants burned alive, and Protestant rulers hanged and quartered Catholics. Moreover, Protestant authorities of one sect jailed and banished Protestants of other sects.

Rather than give up their own faith and accept their sovereign's militant religion, dissenters chose to suffer the privations of the American wilderness, and so a new world got its start. Yet even in the New World there was religious oppression. Quakers were whipped to death in Puritan Massachusetts and those who tried to help them were imprisoned and fined. Not until the end of the seventeenth century did Puritan-dominated Boston give Huguenots, Presbyterians and Anglicans the vote. In other parts of the colonies the Church of England was government-established. All members of dissenting sects paid taxes to the Church, whose ministers preached sermons against dissenters.

No wonder many Americans developed a thorough abhorrence of government-prescribed religion long before the Constitutional Convention. They knew where it led—to persecution, as the group in power struggled to maintain its supremacy. Before they would ratify the Constitution, conventions held in a number of the states demanded that it include a Bill of Rights. As a result, ten amendments were added to the Constitution as soon as it was ratified. These amendments, called the Bill of Rights, guaranteed the citizenry certain rights as a matter of principle—not leaving them up to the whim of the majority. The First Amendment guaranteed freedom of worship, and forbade Congress to make any laws respecting an establishment of religion.

The Founding Fathers knew from bitter personal experience how necessary it was to separate church and state, but their descendants did not always remember. It fell to the Supreme Court, then, to preserve this essential liberty of heart and conscience. This the Court did in a series of cases, one of which, decided on June 17, 1963, was called *Abington Township School District v. Schempp*.

"*Compulsion May Be Subtle*"

The early morning sun slipped in through the broad windows of Abington Township High School near Philadelphia, Pennsylvania. A hush settled over the room. A male teacher sat silently, reverently, facing the long rows of students. Over the public address system a selection from the Bible was being intoned by a young voice.

The words floating down the neat lines of wooden seats hit Ellory Schempp like a slap in the face. For months now Ellory had swallowed his resentment at morning prayer. How dared the public schools regiment him into having to participate in a religious worship that was contrary to his convictions? As a Unitarian Ellory did not believe that the Bible should be taken literally. Consequently, there were many concepts shoved at him during these morning services that went contrary to his faith. Yet, like his parents, Ellory took his church very seriously. He was by nature a sensitive, spiritually conscious youth.

Now he churned inside. Why didn't the public school system pay more attention to the Constitution of the United States? How long had it been since any of the authorities had read the First Amendment, which said, "Congress shall make no laws respecting an establishment of religion, or prohibiting the free exercise thereof"? The Fourteenth Amendment made that principle, and others in the Bill of Rights, binding on the states, as Ellory understood his American history.

The Bible reading over, Abington's Junior class stood and in unison recited the "Lord's Prayer" from the New Testament. And then the class saluted the American flag. The irony of saluting the flag after violating the Constitution made Ellory grimace. Nobody seemed to notice.

His classmates took Ellory's participation very much for granted. They thought of him as a nice-looking boy with light hair who was not too bad an athlete. He liked skiing and mountain climbing, and the class liked him. Nobody, least of all the home room teacher watching these young people, expected Ellory Schempp to be a reformer.

After a few announcements, the teacher dismissed the students and the Junior class cascaded into the hall. Ellory grabbed his books and caught up with his close friends. They were certainly among the brightest students in their year. What, he insisted, did they think of compulsory morning devotion? Several of the boys agreed with Ellory. Yes, the school demanded too much conformity. Probably the Bible reading did violate the Constitution, because Catholics, Protestants and Jews all used different versions of the Scriptures in their own services. Here the school dictated which Bible and which passages they were all to listen to regardless of whether the selection conflicted with any student's own faith.

But the other students did not intend to go along with what Ellory had in mind. Argue with the school authorities! The boys all needed the school's good will to get into college. Besides, they remembered, a state law made the Bible reading compulsory. They had better not try to do anything about it, they decided. Ellory felt he had to do something. He couldn't get the affront out of his mind.

At home Ellory poured out his feelings to his parents. He wanted, he said, to write to an organization called the Civil Liberties Union. They, he hoped, would be interested in helping him protest the state law. Would his parents back him up if he got into a serious fight with the school authorities? Ellory had to know before he went ahead with his plans.

The Schempps were thoughtful. There were two other children in the family to be considered—Donna and Roger. How did they feel about this? Roger, aged fifteen, said little. Donna, aged twelve, was upset. She felt that Ellory was getting the family into trouble. Besides, she did not want to seem different from the other children and be thought an "oddball." Mr. and Mrs. Schempp, respecting both Ellory's and Donna's feelings, were torn. Finally they decided that Ellory could go ahead and protest the school's violation of his religious training. The two younger children would stay out of his protest for the time being.

With his parents behind him, Ellory had all the encouragement he needed. His first problem, he thought, was to put across to the school authorities the idea that they were actually trying to establish what a student's religion should be. It was not long thereafter that a shocked home room teacher found Ellory Schempp during morning devotion reading the Koran—the sacred scriptures of the Moslem faith.

Worse, Ellory did not stand during the Lord's Prayer. When he was questioned, he said that morning devotion violated his conscience. At a loss to understand what had gotten into this otherwise well-behaved boy, the teacher sent Ellory to see the principal. The principal was absent and the vice-principal sent Ellory to talk it over with the guidance counselor. Ellory repeated to the guidance counselor, Miss Brehm, what he had told his home room teacher. He wanted to be excused from morning devotion.

For the remainder of the year 1956–1957 Ellory sat out the devotional period from 8:15 to 8:30 in the guidance counselor's office. The following fall the school decided that it had had enough. The assistant principal sent for Ellory Schempp. Ellory, he said, should stay in his home room and attend devotion "as did the other students."

Ellory boiled inside. He knew that America's greatness had been built by men who put conscience before conformity. He was, however, restrained. The Civil Liberties Union had agreed to help him take his case to court. This hardly seemed the time to get into a fight at school. It would be much better, Ellory reasoned, to wait and see how the court would rule, but court cases take time. The whole of Ellory's Senior year dragged past and he was still reluctantly attending Bible reading and prayer in his home room.

It was August fifth before the Schempp case finally came before a three-judge Federal court and Ellory was called to the witness stand. Nervously, he raised his hand and took the oath to tell the truth. Slowly the Schempps' attorney, Mr. Henry Sawyer, began asking questions.

"How old are you?"

"Eighteen."

Mr. Sawyer then asked Ellory to name the school he had attended. Suddenly it seemed to Ellory there would never be time to pour out all that he felt must be said to the court. First he must describe everything that had happened in the home room. He rattled on.

"Ellory," said Mr. Rhoads, the opposing attorney, "will you be good enough to talk a little more slowly."

"O.K. . . . [It] was an infringement upon my right to think and believe religiously as I wanted to," Ellory explained; ". . . the Bible reading was a religious practice being condoned and forced by the state."

Then, Ellory related, ". . . some discussions ensued between myself and my home room teacher . . . he told me that I should go down and see the principal . . ."

This time it was Judge Biggs who told the anxious youth, "Don't talk so fast." Ellory found it hard not to race his words to cover all he wanted to say. The three judges were in a more leisurely mood. It was to be almost a full year before they ruled.

In the meantime, when school opened in the fall, people all over town were talking about the case. Donna and Roger, of course, became involved. Donna was an honor student and so were most of her friends. They were able to grasp or were told by their parents that the Schempps were fighting for religious liberty, a sacred American principle. Donna's friends remained loyal, but Roger was not so fortunate. He went with a more general group. At least some of them were ignorant of the principles on which their country was founded.

"Bible-hater," they sneered. One day, a group of them driving past the Schempp house in a bus leaned out of the window and yelled, "Commie! Go back to Russia."

The Schempp phone rang all day long. Mrs. Schempp answered each call with infinite patience. To each caller she explained gently that she was not against God or religion. "We're a church-going family," she said. She was, she explained, against having the school dictate what her children's religion should be. In many instances this friendly, talkative woman convinced her caller.

The Schempps were also deluged with mail both for and against them. When the letters were signed, the Schempp family answered them courteously. Finally, in the midst of all the excitement, the three Federal judges, Biggs, Kirkpatrick and Kraft, handed down their decision.

The judges had no doubt that in matters of religious practice Ellory Schempp had the right to be governed by the dictates of his conscience and his own faith. They therefore had to determine whether or not the State of Pennsylvania had attempted to interfere with that right. Had it attempted to establish what religious prac-

tices Ellory was to conform to? Their judgment was that the state
had acted illegally.

The morning devotion period in the public school, the judges
said, was a religious program established by the state. This, in itself,
was unconstitutional. In addition, since the New Testament was
frequently used during these devotions, the state was showing a
preference for the Christian religion. To express their disapproval
of state-prescribed religious practice, the judges cited the decision
of a Supreme Court case: "Neither a State nor the Federal Government can set up a church. Neither can pass laws which aid one
religion, aid all religions, or prefer one religion over another."

The literal acceptance of the words of the Bible is objectionable
to Unitarians, the judges pointed out. Yet the Bible passages had
been read to the students without comment, as if to be taken literally. "Thus strikingly," said the Court, "has the Commonwealth of
Pennsylvania supported the establishment of religion," contrary to
the First Amendment and in violation of the religious tenets of
some of its citizens.

This was exactly what the Founding Fathers had feared—
government backing an established sect or sects—citizens being
told what to believe and how to pray—taxes being collected to
make a man support the propagation of a faith with which he did
not agree. "We hold the statute in issue to be unconstitutional," the
judges concluded.

Their pronouncement sounded final, but their decision hardly
ended the matter. Instead, the Abington Township School District
made elaborate preparations to take the case to the Supreme Court.
Quickly, before the issue could reach the High Court, the Governor
of Pennsylvania caused the state law to be amended. From then on,
if a parent wished, a student could be excused from morning
devotion.

Actually, this change in the statute meant little to the Schempps.
In the new school that Donna and Roger attended, the devotional
service came over a loudspeaker. It was impossible to get away
from it. Besides, any student whose parents wanted him or her
excused was sent to stand in the hall. This was the same procedure
teachers used for punishing children who had not behaved. Donna's
father did not want his sensitive daughter subjected to that embar-
rassment.

Nevertheless the law on the books of the Commonwealth of Pennsylvania had been changed. The Supreme Court justices sent the case back to the three judges of the Federal District Court in Pennsylvania asking that they reconsider their findings in the light of this new development.

The three judges were not impressed by the changes in the law. If the school authorities were to conduct prayers, they needed an audience. "Compulsion" to attend they said, "may be subtle and thus particularly effective in respect to children . . ." Again they quoted from the earlier Supreme Court case of *McCollum v. Board of Education:* "The law of imitation operates, and nonconformity is not an outstanding characteristic of children. The result is an obvious pressure on children to attend."

Evidently they knew what it was like to appear an "oddball" or be called a "Commie" or be segregated and sent into the hall as if you were not part of the group.

Having lost again, the school district people went back to the Supreme Court and once more pleaded to be heard. Then a strange thing happened—something that the Schempps were not a bit happy about. Up from Maryland came another case in which a mother and her high-school-age son objected to morning prayers and Bible reading in Baltimore public schools. Mrs. Murray and her son William were professed atheists. They did not believe in God. As Mrs. Murray explained it, she loved her fellow men and did not get her strength from prayer but from within herself. She believed in good deeds, not in prayers, she said.

The Schempps were disturbed, because atheism is not popular in the United States, and many people even confuse it with Communism, a very different thing. The Murray case made it possible for those who chose to do so to distort the point of the controversy. The Court, they said, if it heard the two cases, would have to decide whether to suppress the majority who wanted to pray, in order to uphold Godless atheists. To the Schempps that was not the point. The point was that they should have the right to choose what kind of spiritual training their children were to have.

This new twist in the issue bothered them. They fully realized that, even if they won their case, a Court's ruling in behalf of religious liberty, to be truly effective, would have to have public support.

The Schempps therefore thought it most unfortunate that the Murrays had managed to get themselves a great deal of publicity and at the same time managed to get themselves thoroughly disliked. Young Murray, the record would indicate, had failed to show much respect toward other people's beliefs. Consequently, a number of his fellow students ganged up to taunt him. Several of these boys discovered Bill one night at the corner drugstore. While shaking something in his face one of them yelled, "I believe! I believe!" Their actions became so threatening that the store owner called the police.

Incidents like this one were distressing even though they bolstered the argument that, by fostering morning prayer, the school was falling down on its basic obligation to teach a cardinal American principle: that in the United States no one ought to tell anyone else what to believe. From the Schempp point of view, Baltimore schools would have turned out better citizens had they, instead of offering a uniform prayer, taught both Bill Murray and his antagonists the great words of Oliver Wendell Holmes: "If there is any principle of the Constitution that more imperatively calls for attachment than any other it is the principle of free thought—not free thought for those who agree with us but freedom for the thought we hate."

Outraged by the abuse of her son, Mrs. Murray took her case against school-fostered worship into the local courts. There she pointed out, as the Schempps had before, that by favoring a program of school prayer the state authorities were making an outcast of anyone who wanted to think differently. Further, she argued that the premium which the school program put on belief in God rendered her beliefs and ideals sinister, alien, and suspect in the eyes of the young people.

Unlike the Federal court in Pennsylvania, the Maryland courts did not uphold this position. Mrs. Murray asked the Supreme Court to review their findings.

The nine justices decided that in their objection to religious observances in schools the two families shared a common legal cause. Therefore, when Mrs. Murray's lawyer asked for the right to be heard, the justices agreed to listen to the arguments in both the Schempp and Murray cases at the same time.

☆

"A Raging Torrent"

The day the Schempp and Murray cases were to be heard the court-room was packed. The spectators rose as the crier signaled the approach of the justices with his familiar, "Oyez, Oyez, Oyez [Hear Ye]! All persons having business before the Honorable, the Supreme Court of the United States are admonished to draw near and give their attention, for the Court is now sitting. God save the United States and this Honorable Court!" Then nine justices, who knew they had an explosive issue on their hands, filed in and took their places on the bench.

Only the year before, the Court had voided a New York prayer written by the Board of Regents for all pupils to repeat. The justices had been emphatic in their decision: " . . . it is not part of the business of government to compose official prayers for any group of the American people to recite as a part of a religious program carried on by the government," they said.

Self-evident though this seemed to many, the decision caused a furor of resentment. "Is the Court putting God out of the schools?" a few people asked.

Emanuel Carlson, writing for the Baptist Committee on Public Affairs, answered tartly, "The person who says that his God has been excluded from the schools by a Court decision thereby professes a very small God." If a teacher or pupil wants to pray at his desk or say grace in the cafeteria before lunch, there is nothing in any Court decision to stop him, he pointed out. "But they must not be ordered to pray."

The last thing the nine Honorable Justices on the bench wanted to do that morning was to stop anyone from praying. The question before them was, rather, whether the state, through the school authorities, could select and direct the prayers of the children, subjecting anyone who did not want to participate to being ostracized— thus segregating children of different faiths under a public school roof.

The school attorneys, by their arguments, showed that they were working hard to justify their clients. Francis B. Burch, arguing for the Baltimore schools, insisted that the use of the Bible and the Lord's Prayer had a salutary effect on the pupils. The morning devotion in school was to instill moral values rather than religious ones, he said.

Associate Justice Arthur Goldberg, the youngest of the justices, interrupted with a question: "Which Bible is used?"

"The King James," said the attorney [although at times other versions were used].

The justices wanted to know whether the attorney's argument would be the same if the Koran were used.

"Yes, sir."

"Then," said Douglas, "it would depend on which group could get control of the school board?"

"I don't think so," said the attorney.

Associate Justice Black, the oldest of the justices, leaned forward and added an inquiry of his own. "You're suggesting that the Constitution gives a local option as to what brand of religion would be taught in the schools?"

The attorney tried to insist that the services in the schools were merely for disciplinary reasons.

This was too much for Justice Black. "How can you say this is not a religious ceremony based on the Christian Bible and their most beloved prayer?" he asked.

Goldberg agreed. He, too, thought the Bible was a religious book.

When the attorneys tried to make the point that services were not compulsory and the students were not forced to attend, Black again was hard to convince. "How," he asked, "can you assume that there is never any pressure on a little child when he has to step aside?"

Chief Justice Warren reminded the advocates that in some school districts in Hawaii the Buddhist faith predominated. He did not say so, but his words implied that if Buddhist ceremonies were conducted daily, Christian children might feel out of place.

Justice Goldberg asked if it would be all right for schools to use the Book of Mormon.

"Yes, sir," said the Maryland lawyer, still sticking to his point.

Black had another question for the attorneys to chew over.

"Some people," he said, "believe that you should not pray in public. Why," he inquired, "should such people not have standing to sue?"

The attorneys insisted that the majority of the parents in their states desired to have their children pray.

What, the justices wanted to know, was to stop a school from taking all its readings from the sacred book of one sect—for example, the Book of Mormon? If prayer and religious reading were allowed, what was going to stop the school from continuing the spiritual indoctrination for most of the day?

At last it was Mr. Henry Sawyer's turn to talk for the Schempps. He was well aware that the justices' questions do not always indicate how they will vote. He was justifiably worried by the ruling the Court had given in an earlier case, the Barnette case.

That controversy had involved children who were Jehovah's witnesses. The boys and girls had refused to salute the American flag because according to their faith it was a graven image. They could not do homage to graven images. The Court ruled that these youngsters could not be forced to violate their consciences. Saluting the flag had to be voluntary. But at the same time the morning ceremony of pledging allegiance continued in the schools.

The Barnette case was different, Sawyer insisted. Saluting the flag was a secular ceremony as far as most children were concerned, and there was no reason why they should not go on with it. In the Schempp case, on the other hand, the rituals objected to were religious. Here, the state was establishing religious worship and giving instruction in faith, breaking down the wall between church and state.

He stressed, too, that in some instances the religious teaching included tenets with which the students' families did not agree. It is not, he argued, to the community's interest to have parents forced to contradict at home and at Sunday school what has been taught in public school. This, Sawyer said, is not the road to good order and discipline among school children.

Here was a fresh argument in the case. The justices retired to consider it, along with all the others they had heard that afternoon; and eventually they met (on a Friday, as usual) to discuss the matter in their oak-paneled, book-lined conference chamber. According to their custom, they shook hands before arranging themselves around the massive table in the middle of the room.

To the left of the Chief Justice sat Justice Potter Stewart, generally conservative. Beyond Stewart sat Justice Arthur Goldberg, a vehement liberal. Then came Justice Byron Raymond White, who, some say, is a man greatly concerned with government authority. To the left of White was Justice John M. Harlan, a conservative who—though gentler and less peppery—thinks in a way that reminds many of old Justice Felix Frankfurter. On Warren's right, in addition to the veterans Clark and Douglas, sat Justice William J. Brennan, tending to be liberal but sometimes, like old Justice Roberts, a swing man. Justice Black sat directly opposite the Chief at the other end of the table.

A portrait of Chief Justice Marshall stared down on the proceedings from above the marble fireplace. It was a fitting ornament. The justices needed the same inner courage Marshall had needed to face up to Jefferson. Their decision was hardly a simple one.

Chief Justice Warren, as always, began the discussion. He spoke solemnly from the head of the table. Then he called on Justice Black, down at the other end of the group. After Black spoke, each of the justices, in turn according to seniority, had a chance to express his views.

All of them except Justice Stewart were convinced that devotional exercises in the public schools were unconstitutional. They must, they decided, uphold the First Amendment and forbid the continuation of such practice. That, however, did not end their problem.

How, the justices wondered, could they put across their decision so that dissenting elements of the population would accept it? Religion is a subject that arouses a great deal of emotion.

Chief Justice Warren assigned the writing of the Court's opinion to Justice Tom Clark, a Presbyterian. Justice William Brennan, a Catholic, and Justice Arthur Goldberg, a Jew, would write separate but concurring opinions. Justice Harlan would concur in Goldberg's opinion, and Justice Douglas was to write still another concurring opinion. Thus the justices intended to put the force of their varied religious and philosophical backgrounds behind the decision. In addition, they decided to announce their findings on the last day of the Court term, June 17, giving the schools the summer to digest the Court's words and to alter their programs.

On the appointed day Clark, sitting on the bench beside the other justices, began quietly, with his Texas drawl, by reviewing the facts of the case. He reminded his listeners that the First Amendment's mandate, "Congress shall make no law respecting an establishment of religion, or prohibiting the free exercise thereof," had been made wholly applicable to the states by the Fourteenth Amendment. Under the First Amendment, the Federal government could not deny the people freedom of speech and freedom of the press, nor deny them freedom of religion. It was, as Clark said, the Fourteenth Amendment that made the First Amendment and these principles binding on the states.

"This freedom of worship was indispensable," the Justice pointed out, "in a country whose people came from the four quarters of the earth and brought with them a diversity of religious opinion. Today, authorities list eighty-three separate religious bodies, each with memberships exceeding fifty thousand, existing among our people, as well as innumerable smaller groups."

Justice Clark pointed out that this was not the first time the Court had reaffirmed the doctrine of complete separation of Church and State and complete religious freedom. He quoted from an earlier case, *Everson v. Board of Education:*

> This freedom was first in the Bill of Rights . . . it was set forth in absolute terms, and its strength is its rigidity. . . . The First Amendment's purpose was . . . to create a complete and permanent separation of the spheres of religious activity and civil authority by comprehensively forbidding every form of public aid or support for religion.

"In short," Justice Clark said, "the Court [in the Everson case] held that the [First] Amendment requires the state to be a neutral in its relations with groups of religious believers and nonbelievers."

Next, Justice Clark reminded everyone how trouble had started in Illinois when religious instructors approved by the superintendent of schools were brought into the schools. A mother, Mrs. McCollum, had protested when children were split up according to their faiths, and sent to separate classrooms for religious instruction. She objected to the use of tax-supported property for such a purpose and claimed that "certain Protestant groups have obtained an overshadowing advantage in the propagation of their faiths over other Protestant sects." Her indignation triggered the McCollum case, decided in 1948.

The Court there held, Clark noted, that "The Constitution . . .

prohibits the government common to all from being embroiled, however innocently, in the destructive religious conflicts of which . . . history . . . records some dark pages."

The relevance of the McCollum case to the present controversy was obvious. No matter what prayer was said in a school, a preference was being shown by the state for the religion from which that prayer was selected. And when a government shows religious preference, it breaches the separation of church and state that the Court is bound to maintain. Nor were the McCollum case and the Everson case the only cases in which the Court had made this clear. There were others, and Justice Clark quoted from them. He then turned his attention to the case at bar.

The attorneys for the two school systems had used as a defense that children could be excused from services. "That fact," said Justice Clark, "furnishes no defense." The very fact that the devotions were officially part of the program of the public schools run by the state constituted the establishment of religious practices by the government. Nor was it a factor that this was a minor breach of the First Amendment. "The breach . . . that is today a trickling stream may all too soon become a raging torrent," he said.

Justice Clark then quoted James Madison: ". . . it is proper to take alarm at the first experiment on our liberties."

The Bible could, of course, be studied objectively as part of a secular program of education. That, the Justice felt, was not what was happening in Maryland or Pennsylvania. In both states it was being used for government-prescribed religious training. This was illegal.

In conclusion, Justice Clark tackled the most difficult argument of them all: what about those who desired to pray and read the Bible in school and their right to do so? Mr. Justice Stewart had sympathized with these people, but Clark explained that freedom of religion could never survive if the majority could use the machinery of the state to spread its beliefs. Everyone was free to worship, but not free to use state facilities to propagate his faith. The very purpose of the Bill of Rights, Clark reminded his listeners, was to take some subjects out of the realm of politics and establish them as principles. One's right to freedom of worship, therefore, depended on no election.

All this protection for the differences in individual conscience is necessary, Justice Clark said, because "The place of religion in our society is an exalted one, achieved through a long tradition of reliance on the home, the church and the inviolable citadel of the individual heart and mind."

That ended the Court's opinion. To it Douglas added that the taxpayers' property was being used to promote morning devotion, and thus all the people were being made to finance a religious exercise that only some of the people wanted—and *"The most effective way to establish any institution is to finance it."* He added, "The First Amendment . . . says that 'no law respecting an establishment of religion' shall be made." This he felt, was clear and conclusive in its relevance to the present cases.

Justice Brennan's opinion was long and learned. In it he advised the schools to establish an atmosphere in which children might assimilate a heritage common to all American groups and religions —a heritage that is simply civic and patriotic. He suggested that good discipline and reverence be instituted not by morning devotion but by reading the great speeches and writings of American patriots.

He sympathized with the children of devout families, like Donna and Roger, who were embarrassed into participating in services contrary to their belief rather than appear "oddballs." He felt that they should not have been put in that position. No child in an American public school should be allowed to feel that because of his religion he is not a complete and full member of the group, Brennan declared. Finally, he reminded his fellow citizens that the Court's ruling in these cases was not new or novel. "The principles which we reaffirm and apply today," he said, "are, in truth, as old as the Republic itself."

Since this case started, the Schempp children have all grown up and gone on to college. Donna has outgrown her sensitiveness and is proud of how her brother stood up for his convictions. Many of the people who disagreed with the Schempps and criticized them for pursuing the case still feel that way. How this story will end depends on how vigilant Americans are in preserving the separation of church and state designed to prevent both faith and government from destroying each other.

Bibliography
Principal Sources, Case 9

UNITED STATES FEDERAL RECORDS—TRANSCRIPTS OF RECORDS AND COPIES OF BRIEFS

Engel v. Vitale, 370 U.S. 421 (1962).

Everson v. Board of Education, 330 U.S. 1 (1947).

McCollum v. Board of Education, 333 U.S. 203 (1948).

Murray v. Curlett, Docket No. 119, Oct. Term 1962. 374 U.S. 203.

"Proposed Amendment to the Constitution Relating to School Prayers and Bible Reading," *A Staff Study for the Committee on the Judiciary House of Representatives* (1964).

School District of Abington Township v. Schempp, Docket No. 142, Oct. Term 1962. 374 U.S. 203.

West Virginia State Board of Education v. Barnette, 319 U.S. 624 (1943).

NEWSPAPERS

Baltimore Sun, June 1, 1963.

New York Times, April 7, 1962, Oct. 6, 1962.

The Atlanta Constitution, March 3, 1963.

The Atlanta Journal, March 3, 1963.

MAGAZINES

"Arguments Before the Court," *United States Law Week* (March 5, 1963).

"Court Rejects Government Sponsorship of Religion," *Report from The Capital,* a bulletin published by the Baptist Joint Committee on Public Affairs (Washington, June–July 1963).

"Should There Be A Constitutional Amendment to Provide Governmental Sponsorship of Religion?" *Report From The Capital,* (Washington, March, 1964).

☆ CASE 10 ☆

Baker v. Carr

The Court Moves to Protect the Value of Every Man's Vote

"Equal representation is so fundamental a principle in a true republic that no prejudice can justify its violation because the prejudices themselves cannot be justified."

THOMAS JEFFERSON, 1819

THE TIMES
AND THE ISSUES

In Black's famous law dictionary the following definition of politics appears: "Pertaining or relating to the policy or the administration of government . . . pertaining to . . . the influence by which individuals of a state seek to determine or control its public policy. . . ."

In such matters of policy the Supreme Court does not interfere. For example, the Court would not rule on whether the United States should recognize the government of another state or nation.

The time, place and manner of holding elections are also matters of policy, and the Constitution has delegated the power to decide those matters to Congress and the state legislatures. Normally the Court would not wish to become involved. But what happens if election districts have been unevenly divided by the state legislature so that the representative of one district speaks for a much smaller population than the representative of another—each nevertheless getting one vote in the United States House of Representatives? Should the Court act to protect the injured voters in the overpopulated sections? This question had to be answered in a series of cases. The key case was called *Baker v. Carr.*

"The Political Thicket"

In America anybody may become a reformer. In *Gibbons v. Ogden* the monopoly was challenged by a ferryboat captain. In the Schempp case religious liberty was championed by a high school youth. In *Brown v. Board of Education of Topeka,* a social revolution was spurred by a Negro preacher. In the fight for a fairer method of choosing state legislatures the principal strategist was Walter Chandler, an elder statesman of the Tennessee Democratic party.

Mr. Chandler's neighbors call him "Captain," remembering that he was a captain in World War I. They remember, too, that throughout the dismal years of the depression he was a United States congressman fighting for measures to speed recovery. During World War II he was mayor of Memphis.

When our story begins in the late 1950's, Chandler, a slim, dark-eyed man of late middle age, was practicing law in the Home Federal Building in Memphis. He thought he had retired from public life, but his imagination was caught by the implications of a novel case in the state courts. The suit did not involve his services but, as Chandler said, "It was a right interesting case." A group of voters led by a man named Gates Kidd had sued to have the state voting districts cut up differently—reapportioned. They had gone into the Court of Chancery complaining that rural people were overrepresented in the state assembly and city people slighted. They showed that as city people they paid more than their share of the state taxes and got less than their share of state money for capital improvements.

What they were doing was like trying to ignite a legal bomb under the state government, and Chandler sympathized. For many decades he had felt that there was no justice in the way Tennessee's voting districts were drawn. The state constitution called for reapportionment every ten years, but the legislature had not redrawn the districting map since 1901. In the more than half a century that had elapsed since then, cities had bulged with a population explosion. At the same time income-hungry farm hands had drifted away from the farms.

Consequently, some sparsely populated areas like Moore County, with little over two thousand inhabitants, elected their own representative to speak and vote their views in the assembly, while other areas like Loudon County, with over thirteen thousand people, had to share a representative with part of another county. A mere forty per cent of the populace—the country slickers—elected sixty-three of the ninety-nine assemblymen, much more than enough to control the legislature. As Chandler figured it, if you lived in a city your vote pretty nearly didn't count. Obviously, that wasn't fair.

Besides, as Chandler reflected, it was not practical to expect the legislature to reform itself. In the past, bills had been introduced to reapportion Tennessee, but they were all killed by the same obstacle. Since the state constitution called for a fixed number of assemblymen, in order to do a really fair job of reapportionment the country districts would have to give up seats in the House to the urban dwellers. Legislators would virtually have to vote themselves out of office and their associates out of political power—and human nature was not like that, as Chandler had learned in his many years of active living.

Going to court, he felt, was a good idea, but the action these fellows had asked the Court of Chancery to take was beyond what that judicial body was willing to do. *Kidd, et al,* had asked the court to order the legislature either to redistrict or have all assemblymen elected at large. In other words, they wanted every citizen to vote for or against any man running for office regardless of his district.

It meant that if there were a few more Democrats than Republicans in the entire state the whole legislature would go Democratic regardless of the Republican majority in some of the counties. It was enough, the court felt, to agree with the petitioners that the state's districting system was out of date and hence unconstitutional. Let the assembly and state senate act on the court's words and reapportion.

That would be fine, Chandler felt, if the legislature obeyed the command. But it didn't. Instead, the state had the Tennessee Attorney General, George F. McCanless, appeal even the finding of the Court of Chancery that the districting was out of date. This was not a proper subject for judicial action, McCanless told the Tennessee Supreme Court. Apportionment, he insisted, was a political question that only the legislature could consider.

But the Tennessee Supreme Court voiced its horror at what it considered would be the ultimate effect of upholding the Court of Chancery and throwing out the apportionment of 1901. "The ultimate result of holding this act unconstitutional," said the Court, ". . . would be to deprive us of the present legislature [elected under it] and of the means of electing a new one." If the men in the assembly were illegally in office, how could they draw up a new voting system? The action of the Court of Chancery, if not overruled, would "bring about the destruction of the state itself." Feeling this way, the Tennessee Supreme Court promptly overruled the lower court.

Walter Chandler, reading the opinion in the case, was too much of a man of action to remain despondent for long. Some time later he decided to pay a call on David N. Harsh, Chairman of Shelby County Commissioners.

"I think I know a way to get past that case," Chandler said. Then he explained that the Tennessee Supreme Court had ruled purely on the state issue. The time, Chandler thought, had come to make this a Federal issue and go into the Federal court. He wanted to claim that since the state districting system provided gross underrepresentation in the state government for certain geographic groups, it thereby denied these groups the equal protection of the law guaranteed them by the Fourteenth Amendment to the United States Constitution.

Harsh was impressed. He and Chandler decided to thrash the idea out with the men at the Memphis city hall. To that end they called a conference. Among those who came were Mayor Edmund Orgill and a Justice of the Peace, Charles W. Baker, who agreed to have his name go on the complaint. As the group was planning to bring its suit against Joe Carr, Secretary of State, using a Justice of the Peace as a plaintiff tickled Chandler's sense of the historic. Here, he said, was the same line-up of combatants as in the old case of *Marbury v. Madison*. He could visualize himself arguing before Chief Justice Marshall. And to Chandler's mind, considering that his fight would revolve around the power of the court to void an unconstitutional act of the legislature, the similarity between the

Baker v. Carr case and the memorable case of 1803 increased. Chandler was having fun.

There was one thing, though, that Chandler felt in all fairness he had to do before going further with his plans. In January of 1959 he wrote every member of the state legislature a letter. In effect it said: There is nothing personal about this, but if you don't redistrict, my clients are prepared to go into Federal court. Chandler believed that it was only sporting to warn them.

Despite the warning, when the legislature adjourned in March it had not redistricted. Promptly Chandler, who is a member of the Memphis Historical Society, started a historic move of his own. He took the question of apportionment into the Federal court. In so doing he was up against one terrible disadvantage that Marbury had not faced in his dispute with Madison. Militating against the Baker case was a 1946 Supreme Court decision in the case of *Colegrove v. Green.*

In the Colegrove suit a political science professor had challenged, not the state legislature, but the congressional districts of his home state of Illinois. Districts varied in size from 112,116 people to 914,053 people, so that a person's vote, the professor figured, was worth only a ninth as much if he lived in the more heavily populated area.

Peppery Justice Frankfurter had spoken for the Court in this early case. The cause, he said, was one of a peculiarly political nature and therefore not proper for judicial interpretation. The Constitution conferred upon Congress exclusive authority to secure fair representation in the popular House, and "If Congress," he said, "failed in exercising its powers, . . . the remedy ultimately lies with the people . . . Courts ought not to enter this political thicket."

The three judges of the Federal district court before whom Chandler brought the *Baker v. Carr* case were well aware of the Colegrove decision. They relied on it heavily in making their own ruling, and referred to it in their explanation of what they had decided. At last they said, "With the plaintiffs' argument that the legislature of Tennessee is guilty of a clear violation of the state constitution and of the rights of the plaintiffs the Court entirely agrees. It also agrees that the evil is a serious one which should be corrected without further delay. But even so, the remedy in this situation clearly does not lie within the courts . . . there are indeed some rights guaranteed by the Constitution for the violation of which the courts cannot give redress. . . ." With that they dismissed the Baker case.

"We'll stick at this case until we win it," Chandler said. In his disappointment, the words of Chief Justice Marshall in the Marbury case came flooding back to him. "The very essence of civil liberty certainly consists in the right of every individual to claim the protection of the laws, whenever he receives an injury." To Chandler, the protection of the law included protection by the courts.

Back in his office he reviewed the Colegrove case and he remembered something very curious about it. For some reason, only seven justices had ruled on that occasion. Only Stanley F. Reed and Harold H. Burton had concurred with Frankfurter that the Court could not rule on a redistricting case. The justice who had swung the Court into denying the professor's demands was Justice Rutledge. Justice Rutledge said the Court had the power to rule on the case. But, he said, it was such a political issue, particularly with an election close at hand, that he thought it would be wiser for the Court not to decide the question. Whenever possible, he added, the Court should avoid handing down fresh interpretations of the Constitution.

As Chandler reread Justice Rutledge's words he felt reassured. The majority of the Supreme Court justices had not foreclosed the possibility of adjudicating a question of unfair representation. Besides, he reasoned, since the Colegrove case had been decided, Reed and Burton had both retired and Earl Warren had become Chief Justice. This was a new Court, this Warren Court. This was a vigorous, forward-looking Court that could break new ground in Constitutional interpretation. This was, after all, the Court that had handed down the order to integrate schools in 1954.

Chandler packed his bags and went to Washington. There he intended to see an attorney who was admitted to bring cases before the Supreme Court bar. Looking for an advocate who was both competent and experienced, he found his way into the office of Charles Rhyne. It was in Rhyne's office that Chandler met Herzel Plaine, an extremely able attorney, then associated with Rhyne and now a Government attorney. The two men, both with keen, alert minds and lively civic concern, enjoyed their association no end.

"How about getting the Supreme Court to take this?" Chandler asked.

Plaine admired the old gentleman's optimism and persistence, but he thought the prospects for getting a Supreme Court hearing were rather gloomy. The big difficulty would be to convince the justices that the Court had jurisdiction over the issue. Unless he could do that, the Court would not agree even to hear their arguments. Plaine was aware that the Court had already refused to review other cases on apportionment.

Everything, he explained, depended on how effective he could make his initial appeal to be heard. The case was up against Frankfurter's objection to seeing the Court involved in "the political thicket."

Fortunately, Chandler had already thought of that problem. To help matters he had seen to it that the co-plaintiffs, with Baker and the other attorneys who had assisted him in the lower courts, came from both the Democratic and the Republican parties and also from several different counties in the state. He was fully conscious that this case must not look like a local political maneuver.

As an additional precaution Chandler and Plaine agreed not to ask the Court to decide what should be done about the unfair districting. If the Supreme Court had to take over the work of the state legislature it probably would refuse the case. The only question Plaine and Chandler decided to put to the Court was whether the judiciary could grant relief in a case of malapportionment. The district court had freely admitted that certain voters were being denied their rights, but the judges thought they were powerless to act. All Chandler and Plaine wanted the Supreme Court to do was decide whether the district court was really powerless or whether it could grant relief to the deprived voter.

To dramatize the urgency of their plea the two attorneys decided to explain that there was now no resort but the Supreme Court for redress of their grievance. The legislature had refused to act. The state court had refused to act. The Federal district court thought itself without authority. Now there was nothing but the Supreme Court to protect the citizen's right to representative government. They might have added Thomas Jefferson's words, "Equal representation is so fundamental a principle in a true republic that no prejudice can justify its violation. . . ."

Plaine did most of the writing of the petition and Chandler said later, "He was wonderful." It was May when Plaine finished that part of the job, and once the petition was sent off to the office of the clerk of the Court there was nothing to do but wait. Four of the justices would have to be convinced by it and vote at a Court conference that they had probable jurisdiction of the issue; otherwise the case was already dead and finished.

On the other hand, Chandler and Plaine realized what might lie ahead if, happily, all went well and the case of *Baker v. Carr* was granted a hearing. Then Plaine and Rhyne would have to get busy and file a written brief stating the case more fully. After that, they would have to wait patiently—possibly for thirty days—while their opponents were given time to file an answer. Then there would be the next wait until there was an opening on the docket and the Court could hear the attorneys. It was Rhyne, the head of the firm, who would give the oral argument and try to win the case if it was to be heard.

All this, though, lay in the future, and all of it depended on the big question: What would the justices say to Plaine's petition? Meanwhile there were plenty of long, suspenseful days ahead. In June the Court adjourned for the hot summer months. Plaine had heard nothing from them. And, as he knew, it would be October before the justices resumed all of their complex duties. Not until barely a month before Christmas did Plaine receive a letter from the clerk of the Court giving the answer to his plea. Holding the letter, he read with a thrill that the justices had indeed noted probable jurisdiction and agreed to hear the arguments.

☆

"Our Oath and Our Office Requires No Less of Us"

It was on Wednesday, April 19, 1961, that the Court heard the Tennessee redistricting case. Dark clouds hung low over the city of Washington and a brisk, damp wind blew. The attorneys, hurrying to the Supreme Court building, found it comfortable to wear their topcoats. Despite the weather Baker's lawyers were in a sunnier

mood than when they had been faced with the unlikely task of persuading the Court to listen to his case. Ever since *Baker v. Carr* had
made the docket, supporting briefs had come flooding in.

Even before that, Mayor Ben West of Nashville—who is said to
have remarked that the legislature "represents more pigs than
people"—had put his city on record as supporting Baker in the
litigation. The Mayor, of course, referred to the overrepresentation
of large tracts of farm land. Now, in addition to West and Nashville, various urban, civic, and taxpayer groups had obtained permission to act as friend of the Court and express their sentiments in
favor of the Court's intervention in districting cases.

Most of these citizens felt as strongly as Chandler. Said one energetic brief, "The Court is here urged to correct one of the most
vicious malignancies in American Government." Nor was that all
the extra help Plaine was getting. The United States government
itself entered the fray when Solicitor General Archibald Cox put in
a brief as friend of the Court.

Cox pointed out that the Court previously had held it illegal
under the Fourteenth Amendment to deny anybody the right to
vote on the basis of his race. Why, he asked, wasn't it just as wrong
to dilute the effect of a citizen's vote because of the geographic
location of his place of residence? He said that the tendency to
favor rural areas in state assemblies was weakening the states.
Municipalities wanting airports, slum clearance, and an elimination
of air pollution, finding themselves outvoted and ignored by their
own state governments, tended to turn to the Federal government
for help in such matters, which might be better attended to locally.
In spite of the outcries of all the civic groups and the effective pleas
by Rhyne and Cox at the end of the arguments, the Court was still
not ready to rule.

Surely the justices were aware of the extent of the problem. In
forty-four states a majority of the legislature could be elected by
less than half the people. In Kansas 19.4% of the population could
select and control the majority of the lower house; in Delaware,
18.5%; in Vermont, 11.9%.

In Connecticut 12% of the people could choose most of the members of the State House of Representatives. Much of the districting
that had been done when Connecticut was still a colony had not
been abolished. As a result, the town of Union, with a population
of 400 people, had two representatives—two voices in the as-

sembly—while at the same time the 162,000 residents of Hartford also had only two representatives and two voices in assembly decisions. These figures were bad enough, but to make matters worse these unrepresentative state legislatures also set Congressional districts, from which Congressmen were elected.

Horrifying though the statistics were, the justices had to face the fact that if the Court undertook to right the injustice it would be deciding how future elections would come out. If the Court made the states equalize the size of districts, population-wise, city folk would be electing more candidates and farmers fewer. The whole political complexion of the country would be changed.

This was a big dose to ask those now in power to swallow. The Court acted cautiously. It took its time. It ordered more arguments on the issue to be heard in the October, 1961, term. Then the justices deliberated among themselves. It was March, 1962, before they finally handed down the first of their many decisions on the apportionment question.

Justice Brennan explained the Court's position. For the time being, the justices had limited their decision to the question of whether a Federal court could grant relief in a malapportionment case—that is, a case where the state voting districts are not equitably drawn. They had decided that it could. For the time being, they were setting no standards as to what a fair districting system should be and making no recommendations as to what relief the lower court should grant. For the time being they left that up to the three judges of the Federal district court in Tennessee. Chandler was told to re-argue his case before them, this time armed with the word of the Supreme Court that district judges had the power to act.

Chandler did successfully re-argue his case and thereby wrung some redistricting reforms out of the legislature, although, in his opinion, not enough. Meanwhile, many people wished the Court had gone further and spelled out what a legal apportionment program should be.

But the justices evidently felt they had given the country's political system a big enough spank for one occasion. Certainly they took note of Justice Frankfurter's rebellious dissent. They knew many people agreed with his words. "This ruling," Frankfurter said, was a "massive repudiation of the experience of our whole past." The Court should stay out of politics. He called it an assertion of destructively novel judicial power. In addition he felt that since the Court had set no standards as to how districts should be organized, it had merely triggered off a host of law suits to plunge the lower courts into a mathematical bog.

Justice Frankfurter, who was about to retire, was right about one thing. Far from settling the controversy, *Baker v. Carr* only gave it a start. By December, 1963, court, legislative, or referendum action on the question of state districting had gone on in forty-two states. And all the arguing litigants and all the debating legislators were plagued by the many puzzles left unanswered by the Court.

Politicians battled over such questions as how much malapportionment could be legal. Wasn't it permissible, if a state's lower house was based on population, for the state senate to represent unequal geographical districts? After all, the Federal government is run this way. Couldn't a state keep a system of unequal representation if the people voted by referendum to do so? Besides these, there were other issues discussed with equal spirit.

In Virginia a slim, elderly attorney named Edmund D. Campbell shocked his robust partner, Hugh Obear, when he became the counsel for a group of Virginia state legislators who decided to take advantage of the Supreme Court decision in *Baker v. Carr*. Since the legislature refused to reapportion, they were going into Federal court.

Obear charged into Campbell's neat, sparely furnished office, arguing as partners do. He pointed a fat finger across the desk at his seated partner and declared, "I don't like this invasion of the rights of the states." In an accusing tone he added, "You're a Federalist! You believe in great sweeping powers for the Federal government."

"I'm not," Campbell shook his head. "I'm a Jeffersonian Republican." He didn't like being compared to Chief Justice Marshall. "I believe in local government wherever it's possible," he insisted. "I'm trying to strengthen the state." He meant it. A loyal Virginian, he firmly believed that when Virginia's populated areas got fairer representation Virginia would move forward. He liked to remind people that Virginia once led the nation in concepts of government and he would love to see that—for him—happy state of affairs return. Unfortunately he wasn't able to put all this across to his partner.

Eventually the Virginia case reached the Supreme Court and Campbell had plenty of company. Attorneys from Alabama, New York, Colorado and Maryland were also bringing their state districting feuds before the Court. Cases from nine other states were awaiting a place on the docket.

The justices probably smiled to themselves. The number of cases coming from voters who were prepared to show they had been discriminated against proved the need for the Court's earlier action. That should help to quiet the Court's critics.

In June, 1964, the justices diligently set about settling the problems that all these agitated litigants brought before them. In so doing they were aided by two decisions they had handed down since *Baker v. Carr*. One of these, *Gray v. Sanders,* involved the State of Georgia's primary elections for statewide office. Here again, the overpopulated neighborhoods had been at a disadvantage. In throwing out the system the Supreme Court said, ". . . all who participate in an election are to have an equal vote—whatever their race, whatever their sex, whatever their occupation, whatever their income, and wherever their home may be in the geographical unit." Put in other words, their statement meant, "One person, one vote"!

Here was one standard to guide the confused communities trying to redistrict. Soon the Georgia primary story had a sequel. In Atlanta a group of dashing young men, all under thirty, read the Court's decision. They decided that if primaries had to be fair, why not Congressional elections? Under the leadership of an attorney just out of Harvard, and a youthful accountant named James P. Wesberry, Jr., they brought their case against Governor Sanders and took it all the way up to the Supreme Court.

The Court took a look at Georgia's "crazy quilt" districting and laid down a second dramatic standard for apportionment. As nearly as practical, they said, Congressional districts as set by the state legislature must be equal in population.

Justice Harlan's dissent reverberated with the shock he was experiencing. "I had not expected to witness the day," he said, "when the Supreme Court of the United States would render a decision which cast grave doubt on the constitutionality of the composition of the House of Representatives. It is not an exaggeration to say that such is the effect of today's decision."

He estimated that under the ruling, 398 representatives from 37 states were not entitled to their seats. He then claimed that, as the states could set voting qualifications, they could also decide the size of districts.

Justice Stewart also felt the Court had gone beyond the dictates of the Constitution. Nevertheless, the Court had ruled, and five days later Georgia was redistricted.

Reporters, meanwhile, saw the smoke of a fight between Court and Congress. Wouldn't every representative whose seat was now in danger be on edge to do something to limit the effect of the Court's action? They hurried to the Capitol to find out. At the time, the reporters were disappointed. The storm came later. Many congressmen then (as later) took the position that reapportionment was necessary but it was too bad that it had taken the Supreme Court to do something about it. Many of them wished that they themselves had passed legislation to correct the problem before it became a Court case. Others wanted to take such cases away from the Court completely.

With this background the justices, in June of 1964, faced the mass of cases brought by Campbell and the others. All of them involved districting for state elections. To all of them the Court applied the same principles used in the Georgia primary case and in the Georgia redistricting case: districts should have equal population and each person should have one vote. In addition the Court answered another vital query.

In Colorado a state-wide referendum had approved a districting plan which deprived the voters of Denver of a fair voice in the state senate. A group of civic-minded citizens led by a man named Lucas wanted to know if this was legal. No, the justices said. A person's vote was a very personal thing and its value could not be diluted, even by referendum.

At the same time the Court ruled on the whole question of state senators. They could not be selected from geographical districts of vastly different numbers of voters, the Court said. The justices were dismayed that in Maryland 14.2 per cent of the population could elect a controlling number of the state senators; in Nevada, 8 per cent; in California, 10.7 per cent; in Idaho, 16.6 per cent of the people.

Most of the justices wanted to put an end to this.

Districts had to be about equal in population, they declared through Warren's statement. On hearing this part of the decision, Obear took his partner, Campbell, to task. "I cannot see," he said, "why what's good enough for the Federal government isn't good enough for the states."

Chief Justice Warren had already answered Obear, in his state-

ment of the Court's opinion. There was no comparison, he said, between a state senate and the United States Senate. The Federal
government was formed by a group of once-independent states,
and " a compromise between the larger and the smaller states . . .
averted a deadlock . . . which had threatened to abort the birth of
our nation." This compromise allowed the people to be represented
in the House and the states to be represented in the United States
Senate. Parts of a state, counties or farms, had never been sovereign
entities. They did not have to be lured into the body politic. A state
senate should not be so constituted as to permit a minority to
thwart the will of the majority.

Six justices concurred in all these decisions. Justice Clark and
Justice Stewart had some reservations. Justice Stewart said he did
not feel that all Congressional districts had to be equal in population. Both he and Clark questioned the ruling that seats in *both*
houses of a State legislature have to be allocated to districts of
equal populations. Districts, they felt, need only be rational in design and not a "crazy quilt."

Justice Harlan once more gave a strongly emotional dissent. The
Court, he felt, should not be a "general haven for reform move-
ments." The Court was taking on too much—jeopardizing its own
future as the unquestioned voice of the Constitution.

Whether they agreed with Harlan or with the majority, voters all
over the land were shaken by the political importance of this decision. The Court, by judicial decree, had redistributed American
political power. As a result of this decision old forces would tumble
in the elections ahead. Eventually new groups, more urban in composition, would seize the reins of government. Some said the states
would be stronger and do more for themselves; others claimed that
legislators, both local and national, would be more progressive.
There were those who predicted that the Negro would get more
consideration.

The reapportionment cases are exciting because they are a part
of a growing pattern—a pattern of protecting the individual's rights
in a crowded world.

Many of the Court's actions are typical of this pattern. In 1963,
in the now-famous Gideon case, the Court ruled that a poor man
accused of a crime had to be provided with an attorney to defend
him. Usually this means someone appointed by the Court. In
addition to ordering redistricting and faster school integration, the

Supreme Court in 1964 unanimously moved to extend freedom of speech and the press. It struck down a libel suit against the *New York Times* for criticizing law enforcement in Montgomery, Alabama. Newspapers and private citizens are now freer than ever before to criticize their government.

That same year the Court further extended the mandates of the Bill of Rights as applied to the states. It held that the Fifth Amendment, which guarantees that no one accused of a crime can be made to testify against himself, was as applicable to state trials as to Federal ones.

No decision made by an umpire ever pleased everyone. Inevitably, there are those who say the Court is moving at too fast a pace, blazing too many new trails, exercising its awesome might in too many areas. The justices, they argue, are appointed for life, not elected. They should, therefore, be strictly limited in power.

To answer them, the friends of the Court point out that the justices are only fulfilling the function bequeathed them by the Founding Fathers—to protect the individual's right against intrusion by society. The Court is shielding the little man against bigness. It is preserving liberty in an age when the tendency is to forfeit the individual's rights for the convenience of the group. Friends of the Court feel that it is a healthy thing that the public and the other departments of Government, both executive and legislative, still know that when a citizen is imposed upon, the Court is there to protect him. They point out that Congress and the states could have done the work of redistricting on their own, as in England, where the "rotten boroughs" with almost no population were eliminated by Parliament over a century ago. In America, when Congress and the states had failed to act, the Court came to the rescue of millions of injured voters.

As Chief Justice Warren himself expressed it, "We are cautioned about the dangers of entering the political thickets . . . Our answer is this: A denial of constitutionally protected rights demands judicial protection; our oath and our office requires no less of us."

In so speaking he merely reiterated the edicts of Chief Justice Marshall declaring the right of every injured individual to claim the protection of the law. As Marshall said, "It is emphatically the province and duty of the judicial department to say what the law is."

Protecting the injured by announcing the law in accordance with the mandates set forth in the Constitution is exactly what the Court is still doing. Like Marshall the justices are forever mindful that it is a Constitution that they are interpreting—not a detailed legal code, but a set of basic, fundamental principles. It makes no difference, as Marshall explained, that the word "bank" does not appear in the document. Congress can still charter a bank if by so doing it is carrying out one of its legitimate functions. Nor does it matter that the framers of the Fourteenth Amendment made no mention of integrated schools. They fully intended to initiate a program of freedom and equality for all men under the law. And schools, since that Amendment was passed, have become so important that only through their integration can Negroes enjoy equal citizenship and have an equal opportunity to succeed. Therefore, the Constitution requires an end to segregation. The justices now, as of old, must decide what essential values the Founding Fathers intended to protect.

This they must do in a world that is infinitely more complex, more crowded, more highly organized and more filled with conflicts than in the days of Marshall. Only through their vigilance can the Constitution remain in operation. Only through their broad understanding can its principles of liberty and justice for all survive. Only with the support of an informed and loyal public can the justices continue to preserve every man's rights and every man's liberties. The Court wields neither the power of the purse nor the power of the sword; it controls neither the Army nor the Treasury. To keep us a free people it relies on the dedication of American citizens to their own legacy. They inherited a self-governing nation which can only rest on a belief in the dignity of all mankind and the worth of the private citizen. To perpetuate these principles we rely on the Court, and the Court must rely on all of us.

Bibliography
Principal Sources, Case 10

BOOKS

Black, Henry Campbell, *Black's Law Dictionary*. St. Paul, Minn. 1933.

UNITED STATES FEDERAL RECORDS—TRANSCRIPTS OF RECORDS AND COPIES OF THE BRIEFS

Baker v. Carr, 369 U.S. 186 (1962).

Colegrove v. Green, 328 U.S. 549 (1946).

Davis v. Mann, Docket No. 69, Oct. Term 1963. 377 U.S. 678.

Gray v. Sanders, 372 U.S. 368 (1963).

Lucas v. The Forty-Fourth General Assembly of Colorado, Docket No. 508, Term 1963. 377 U.S. 713.

Reynolds v. Sims, Docket No. 23, Oct. Term 1963. 377 U.S. 533.

The Maryland Committee for Fair Representation v. Tawes, Governor of Maryland, Docket No. 29, Oct. Term 1963. 377 U.S. 656.

Wesberry v. Sanders, Docket No. 22, Oct. Term 1963. 376 U.S. 1.

Gideon v. Wainwright, 372 U.S. 335 (1963).

NEWSPAPERS

New York Herald Tribune, Feb. 23, 1964.

New York Times, Feb. 18, 1964; Feb. 23, 1964; June 16, 21 and 29, 1964.

Washington Post, June 16, 1964.

MAGAZINES

Congressional Quarterly, March 26, 1962; December 27, 1963; June 19, 1964.

APPENDIX

Justices of the Supreme Court
and Their Terms of Office

F. Federalist   *D. Democrat*   *R. Republican*

APPOINTED BY PRESIDENT WASHINGTON, Federalist from Virginia (1789–1797)

John Jay, F., N.Y. (1789–1795), *First Chief Justice.*
John Rutledge, F., S.C. (1789–1791).
William Cushing, F., Mass. (1789–1810).
James Wilson, F., Pa. (1789–1798).
John Blair, F., Va. (1789–1796).
James Iredell, F., N.C. (1790–1799).
Thomas Johnson, F., Md. (1791–1793).
William Paterson, F., N.J. (1793–1806).
John Rutledge, F., S.C. (1795). *Chief Justice.*
Samuel Chase, F., Md. (1796–1811).
Oliver Ellsworth, F., Conn. (1796–1800), *Chief Justice.*

APPOINTED BY PRESIDENT ADAMS, Federalist from Massachusetts (1797–1801)

Bushrod Washington, F., Va. (1789–1829).
Alfred Moore, F., N.C. (1799–1804).
John Marshall, F., Va. (1801–1835), *Chief Justice.*

APPOINTED BY PRESIDENT JEFFERSON, Republican from Virginia (1801–1809)

William Johnson, R., S.C. (1804–1834).
Brockholst Livingston, R., N.Y. (1806–1823).
Thomas Todd, R., Ky. (1807–1826).

APPOINTED BY PRESIDENT MADISON, Republican from Virginia (1809–1817)
    Gabriel Duval, R., Md. (1811–1835).
    Joseph Story, R., Mass. (1811–1845).

APPOINTED BY PRESIDENT MONROE, Republican from Virginia (1817–1825)
    Smith Thompson, R., N.Y. (1823–1843).

APPOINTED BY PRESIDENT ADAMS, Republican from Massachusetts (1825–1829)
    Robert Trimble, R., Ky. (1826–1828).

APPOINTED BY PRESIDENT JACKSON, Democrat from Tennessee (1829–1837)
    John McLean, D. (later R.), Ohio (1829–1861).
    Henry Baldwin, D., Pa. (1830–1844).
    James M. Wayne, D., Ga. (1835–1867).
    Roger B. Taney, D., Md. (1836–1864), *Chief Justice.*
    Philip P. Barbour, D., Va. (1836–1841).

APPOINTED BY PRESIDENT VAN BUREN, Democrat from New York (1837–1841)
    John Catron, D., Tenn. (1837–1865).
    John McKinley, D., Ky. (1837–1852).
    Peter V. Daniel, D., Va. (1841–1860).

APPOINTED BY PRESIDENT TYLER, Whig from Virginia (1841–1845)
    Samuel Nelson, D., N.Y. (1845–1872).

APPOINTED BY PRESIDENT POLK, Democrat from Tennessee (1845–1849)
    Levi Woodbury, D., N.H. (1845–1851).
    Robert C. Grier, D., Pa. (1846–1870).

APPOINTED BY PRESIDENT FILLMORE, Whig from New York (1850–1853)
    Benjamin R. Curtis, W., Mass. (1851–1857).

APPOINTED BY PRESIDENT PIERCE, Democrat from New Hampshire (1853–1857)
    John A. Campbell, D., Ala. (1853–1861).

APPOINTED BY PRESIDENT BUCHANAN, Democrat from Pennsylvania (1857–1861)
> Nathan Clifford, D., Me. (1858–1881).

APPOINTED BY PRESIDENT LINCOLN, Republican from Illinois (1861–1865)
> Noah H. Swayne, R., Ohio (1862–1881).
> Samuel F. Miller, R., Iowa (1862–1890).
> David Davis, R. (later D.), Ill. (1862–1877).
> Stephen J. Field, D., Cal. (1863–1897).
> Salmon P. Chase, R., Ohio (1864–1873), *Chief Justice.*

APPOINTED BY PRESIDENT GRANT, Republican from Illinois (1869–1877)
> William Strong, R., Pa. (1870–1880).
> Joseph P. Bradley, R., N.J. (1870–1892).
> Ward Hunt, R., N.Y. (1872–1882).
> Morrison R. Waite, R., Ohio (1874–1888), *Chief Justice.*

APPOINTED BY PRESIDENT HAYES, Republican from Ohio (1877–1881)
> John Marshall Harlan, R., Ky. (1877–1911).
> William B. Woods, R., Ga. (1880–1887).

APPOINTED BY PRESIDENT GARFIELD, Republican from Ohio (Mar.–Sept. 1881)
> Stanley Matthews, R., Ohio (1881–1889).

APPOINTED BY PRESIDENT ARTHUR, Republican from New York (1881–1885)
> Horace Gray, R., Mass. (1881–1902).
> Samuel Blatchford, R., N.Y. (1882–1893).

APPOINTED BY PRESIDENT CLEVELAND, Democrat from New York (1885–1889)
> Lucius Q. C. Lamar, D., Miss. (1888–1893).
> Melville W. Fuller, D., Ill. (1888–1910), *Chief Justice.*

APPOINTED BY PRESIDENT HARRISON, Republican from Indiana (1889–1893)
> David J. Brewer, R., Kans. (1889–1910).
> Henry B. Brown, R., Mich. (1890–1906).
> George Shiras, R., Pa. (1892–1903).
> Howell E. Jackson, D., Tenn. (1893–1895).

APPOINTED BY PRESIDENT CLEVELAND, Democrat from New York (1893–1897)
> Edward D. White, D., La. (1894–1910).*
> Rufus W. Peckham, D., N.Y. (1895–1909).

APPOINTED BY PRESIDENT McKINLEY, Republican from Ohio (1897–1901)
> Joseph McKenna, R., Cal. (1898–1925).

APPOINTED BY PRESIDENT ROOSEVELT, Republican from New York (1901–1909)
> Oliver Wendell Holmes, R., Mass. (1902–1932).
> William R. Day, R., Ohio (1903–1922).
> William H. Moody, R., Mass. (1906–1910).

APPOINTED BY PRESIDENT TAFT, Republican from Ohio (1909–1913)
> Horace H. Lurton, D., Tenn. (1909–1914).
> Charles E. Hughes, R., N.Y. (1910–1916).†
> Edward D. White, promoted from associate justiceship. Served (1910–1921) as *Chief Justice*.
> Willis Van Devanter, R., Wyo. (1910–1937).
> Joseph R. Lamar, D., Ga. (1910–1916).
> Mahlon Pitney, R., N.J. (1912–1922).

APPOINTED BY PRESIDENT WILSON, Democrat from New Jersey (1913–1921)
> James C. McReynolds, D., Tenn. (1914–1941).
> Louis D. Brandeis, D., Mass. (1916–1939).
> John H. Clarke, D., Ohio (1916–1922).

APPOINTED BY PRESIDENT HARDING, Republican from Ohio (1921–1923)
> William H. Taft, R., Conn. (1921–1930), *Chief Justice*.
> George Sutherland, R., Utah (1922–1938).
> Pierce Butler, D., Minn. (1922–1939).
> Edward T. Sanford, R., Tenn. (1923–1930).

APPOINTED BY PRESIDENT COOLIDGE, Republican from Massachusetts (1923–1929)
> Harlan F. Stone, R., N.Y. (1925–1941).‡

* Later appointed Chief Justice by Taft.
† Later appointed Chief Justice by Hoover.
‡ Later appointed Chief Justice by Roosevelt.

APPOINTED BY PRESIDENT HOOVER, Republican from California (1929–1933)

> Charles E. Hughes, promoted from associate justiceship. Served (1930–1941) as *Chief Justice.*
> Owen J. Roberts, R., Pa. (1930–1945).
> Benjamin N. Cardozo, D., N.Y. (1932–1938).

APPOINTED BY PRESIDENT ROOSEVELT, Democrat from New York (1933–1945)

> Hugo L. Black, D., Ala. (1937–   ).
> Stanley F. Reed, D., Ky. (1938–1957).
> Felix Frankfurter, Ind., Mass. (1939–1962).
> William O. Douglas, D., Conn. (1939–   ).
> Frank Murphy, D., Mich. (1940–1949).
> James F. Byrnes, D., S.C. (1941–1942).
> Harlan F. Stone, promoted from associate justiceship. Served (1941–1946) as *Chief Justice.*
> Robert H. Jackson, D., N.Y. (1941–1954).
> Wiley B. Rutledge, D., Iowa (1943–1949).

APPOINTED BY PRESIDENT TRUMAN, Democrat from Missouri (1945–1953)

> Harold H. Burton, R., Ohio (1945–1958).
> Fred M. Vinson, D., Ky. (1946–1953), *Chief Justice.*
> Tom C. Clark, D., Tex. (1949–   ).
> Sherman Minton, D., Ind. (1949–1956).

APPOINTED BY PRESIDENT EISENHOWER, Republican from New York (1953–1961)

> Earl Warren, R., Cal. (1953–   ), *Chief Justice.*
> John M. Harlan, R., N.Y. (1955–   ).
> William J. Brennan, D., N.J. (1956–   ).
> Charles E. Whittaker, R., Mo. (1957–1962).
> Potter Stewart, R., Ohio (1958–   ).

APPOINTED BY PRESIDENT KENNEDY, Democrat from Massachusetts (1961–1963)

> Arthur J. Goldberg, D., Ill. (1962–   ).
> Byron R. White, D., Colo. (1962–   ).

Suggestions for Further Reading

BIOGRAPHIES

Bowen, Catherine Drinker, *Yankee From Olympus*, Little Brown (1944). A thoroughly enjoyable history of Associate Justice Oliver Wendell Holmes, his family and career.

Loth, David G., *Chief Justice; John Marshall and the Growth of the Republic*. W. W. Norton and Company (1949). A readable account of Marshall in relation to his times.

Medina, Harold R., *Anatomy of Freedom*. Henry Holt and Co. (1959). A highly interesting collection of articles by the judge who tried a sensational Communist conspiracy case.

Mendelson, Wallace, Editor, *Felix Frankfurter, a Tribute,* William Morrow (1964). A number of distinguished citizens give their impressions of the Justice in this collection.

Perkins, Dexter, *Charles Evans Hughes and American Democratic Statesmanship*. Little Brown (1956). A short and meaty biography of Hughes and his work.

Pringle, Henry F., *The Life and Times of William Howard Taft*. Farrar and Rinehart (1939). This author won a Pulitzer prize for his biography of Theodore Roosevelt. The last eight chapters of Volume II of the Taft biography give a picture of Taft's life on the bench.

Williams, Charlotte, *Hugo L. Black: a Study in the Judicial Process,* Johns Hopkins Press (1950). Black, a controversial appointee because of a mistake he made in his youth, goes on to make a brilliant record as a Supreme Court Justice.

GENERAL

Acheson, Patricia, *The Supreme Court—America's Judicial Heritage,* Dodd, Mead (1961). Mrs. Acheson deals with the place of the Court in American history.

Barth, Alan. *The Heritage of Liberty,* Webster Publishing Co., (1965). An excellent history of civil liberties intended for high school use. Distributed by the Center for Information on America, Washington, Connecticut.

Clayton, James E., *The Making of Justice—The Supreme Court in Action.* E. P. Dutton (1964). This book takes the reader through the activities in a typical year in Court history, and is written in a lively style.

Garraty, John A., ed., *Quarrels That Have Shaped the Constitution.* Harper & Row (1962). This book gives a brief picture of sixteen Supreme Court Cases, many of which are covered in the present volume.

Jackson, Robert H. *The Supreme Court in the American System of Government.* Harvard University Press. (1955). The late Supreme Court Justice Jackson's valuable and informative book on the high court.

Lewis, Anthony, *Gideon's Trumpet,* Random House (1964). The exciting history of an important criminal case decided by the Supreme Court, along with vivid details of how the Court operates.

McCloskey, Robert G., *The American Supreme Court.* University of Chicago Press (1960). This is a careful study of the Supreme Court by a well-known scholar.

Prettyman, Barrett, Jr., *Death and the Supreme Court.* Harcourt, Brace and World, Inc. (1961). Here are six gripping case histories of criminal cases that reached the Supreme Court. The author introduces us to Court procedures and gives us an inside view of the justices at work.

Swisher, Carl Brent, *Historic Decisions of the Supreme Court,* Van Nostrand (1958). A number of important cases are presented in brief. This author has also written other well-recommended books on the Court.

Tresolini, Rocco J., *Justice and the Supreme Court.* Lippincott (1963). This is a book for young people. It gives a few cases and little sketches of the justices who decided them.

Index

THE AUTHOR

MARJORIE FRIBOURG was born in a 150-year-old house in Chappaqua, New York. At an early age she "exhibited a marked ability for elaborate storytelling" which she believes explains why most of her earlier works were fiction. A graduate of Columbia University Teachers College, she has taught off and on through the years and read her husband's law books avidly to get a better background in American history. In doing research for an earlier nonfiction assignment, she discovered to her joy that her experience in writing fiction could help to bring alive the vivid, true-life experiences behind great historical events.

Finding her own old Constitutional Law case book hopelessly outdated and lacking in personal details, she spent most of the past two years in the Library of Congress, tracking down the elusive human element of the great Supreme Court cases through the law library, the newspaper room, the stacks behind the main reading room, and the rare book collection. Some of her material came from the National Archives and from conversations with participants in the more recent cases. She has thoroughly enjoyed the search. A resident of Washington, where her husband is a trial examiner with the Federal Power Commission, Mrs. Fribourg has kept up an active membership in national civic and literary organizations.